Channels of Healing

STUDIES FOR THE PEOPLE OF GOD

Owen Dowling

Speedwell Press

Channels of Healing: Studies for the People of God
By Owen Dowling

Editor: Paul Nockleby
Cover art: Steven Hallam
Cover design: Dawn Mathers

1   2   3   4   5   6   7   8   9   10   11   12   13   14   15   16

Contents

Introduction

Channels of Healing has been written to encourage Christian believers and seekers to become involved in healing ministry. Many have prayed in the spirit of the prayer of St Francis of Assisi: 'Lord make me an instrument of your peace'. It is also quite appropriate to pray: 'Lord make me a channel of your healing and wholeness.' In the following studies we discover that the people of God are encouraged to pray and act in the name and spirit of Jesus Christ, for the healing of souls and bodies. We can be channels of God's healing.

Each study is relatively short and encourages us to look at some biblical material and apply it in the here and now. There are questions for reflection or discussion at the conclusion of each study. They can be used individually or corporately, for example, in a home Bible study discussion group, an Order of St Luke Chapter, or in private prayer and meditation. There are thirty studies; a group or chapter which meets once per month could use ten studies per year over a three-year period.

Over the years of my own ministry I have been encouraged to step out in healing ministry—to put into action in the particular what I believe in general. I have sought to encourage believers and clergy to step out in this ministry themselves and trust that these studies will be a continuing means of such encouragement. Jesus commissioned the church to heal in his name, and it should be normal for any congregation not only to have a ministry of intercessory prayer for those needing healing, but also to have laying on of hands and anointing services for the healing of the sick. I believe that God is a healing God, as the scriptures teach, and that Jesus Christ and the Holy Spirit mediate this healing to us. I know that 'Jesus saves' can equally be translated as 'Jesus heals'.

Along with the Order of St Luke, however, I respect the work of medical doctors, nurses, paramedics, counsellors, pharmacists, and medical science. Though medical personnel may or may not believe in God or think of God as directing their work, God uses them as agents of healing and they are part of God's gift to us. We also know that prayer ministry together with the loving, caring support of a faith community can greatly enhance or strengthen the effect of medical treatment. As a singer and musician I also believe that praise, thanksgiving and even lament can help to heal us in our spirit, if not in our body. My conviction is that some blessing flows whenever we pray and minister in Christ's name, though it may not be always the blessing we seek or expect. There are times of great disappointment or dark places we go through when we simply don't have answers. Our disappointment or darkness, however, should not discourage us from continuing to seek God's help, even when we are in the most extreme circumstances.

Included at the end of the book is an address which I gave to the Order of St Luke in Victoria, Australia, in May of 2001. This address contains a number of observations on my own journey in healing ministry, and including it here may give opportunity for people to discuss certain issues which arise for them relating to involvement in this ministry. It is my joy and determination to go on ministering, teaching and writing about Christian healing as long as there is breath in me.

Owen Dowling
Canberra, September 2005

1

A Healthy Doctrine of Creation

Readings: Genesis 1:1 - 2:3; John 5:15-18

The Bible begins with a very strong statement of the goodness of God's creation. It is a healthy creation—health and wholeness are built into it. 'God saw everything that he had made, and indeed it was very good' (Genesis 1:31). God is pictured in a human way, as sitting back, resting for a full day, and surveying his handiwork.

In our often unwise and exploitative ways we have destroyed many of the balances and intricate interdependencies of the wonderful creation in which we are placed. The Genesis stories remind us that we have to assume a responsible place in God's creation, and not abuse it. Otherwise it will turn to a desert and place of our own destruction, bringing forth thorns and thistles and much pain and suffering.

One way of exercising responsibility within God's creation is to look after our own minds and bodies—to give them a healthy diet and keep a good balance between work and rest and recreation. We certainly need our own day of rest and reflection as well as days of useful work. The sabbath principle is a principle of health.

All healing ministry is based on belief that God is the Creator and re-Creator. What God made, God can remake. The word 'recreation' itself implies that we are restored to health and remade by God during times of rest and relaxation, when we have opportunity to enjoy life and rejoice as creatures in God's creation.

It can be said that to engage in worship—the praise of God in creation—is a healthy thing. Worship releases something health-giving in us, in the cells of our body and in the anxious convolutions of our mind.

Though God is pictured, symbolically speaking, as resting on the concluding day of creation and rejoicing in the completeness of it all, there is a sense in which creation is on-going. God is always creating and recreating.

It is interesting that this is the way Jesus sees God. In John's gospel, Jesus says: 'My Father is still working, and I also am working' (John 5: 17). Jesus had been criticized for healing a paralyzed man on the sabbath. On another sabbath day he used spittle and clay and spread mud on a blind man's eyes to heal him, a reminder of the work of God the Creator, who formed us human beings from the dust of the earth (see Genesis 2:7).

Traditional Jewish belief was that the Messiah, when he came, would do works of healing on the sabbath. The Messiah would be known to God's people from his healing on the sabbath, and this would link him with God the continuing creator. As Jesus performed works of healing on the sabbath, he caused much offense, as people around Jesus could see who he was claiming to be.

Jesus calls us to link ourselves with God the Creator and re-Creator. When we pray and lay hands or anoint in Jesus' name, we can think of ourselves as drawing on, focusing and channeling the creative power of God. The molecules jump faster. We are stirring up the healing, creative energies in the person we are praying for; we are engaged, with Jesus, in the work of healing and recreation. He gives us a part to play in God's continuing work.

For Thought and Discussion

1. Think about the goodness of creation. What are some of the things you marvel at?

2. What signs are there of healing properties inherent in creation?

3. Compose a prayer which you could pray for yourself or for another person who needs healing, using insights gained from this study.

4. In what way is the sabbath commandment ("Remember the sabbath day to keep it holy") beneficial for health?

2

Blame is the Game

Reading: Genesis 3:1-13

In this ancient story of Adam and Eve there is a depiction of human sin and rebellion against God and the wholeness of being and relationship which he plans for us. Perhaps it's a story more about the breaking of relationships between God and humanity and between human beings themselves than it is a story about the origins of the human race. Certainly it is about all human beings; Adam and Eve are clearly representative of us all.

Adam and Eve are tempted by the serpent to disobey God. Temptation is subtle; it sneaks up on us and cleverly insinuates itself into our patterns of thought. In the Hebrew Bible (the Old Testament) spiritual and psychological truths are often described concretely—in symbol, metaphor and story. Jesus was an inheritor of this tradition and spoke God's truths that way. That's why people loved to listen to him—he was so vivid in his way of speaking.

The serpent suggests to Adam and Eve that if they reach out to pluck and eat the fruit of the knowledge of good and evil—ultimate divine knowledge—they will be like God. This is the basic sin of human pride. We don't want God to be our helper and guide—the one wiser than us. We want to be in total control ourselves.

The result of human rebellion is first of all a break in relationship with God. Adam and Eve hide themselves in the garden. They know that they are naked (a vivid way of describing their sense of guilt and vulnerability). They are afraid of God and he has to search for them. 'Where are you?' It's a game of hide and seek which human beings play with God and one another. We hide from the knowledge of ourselves and what we have done.

Then there is a break of relationship between the man and the woman. The blame game begins. God asks Adam whether he has eaten of the fruit he was told not to eat. The man immediately blames the woman (and God too, because he had given him the woman as his companion). 'The woman whom you gave to be with me, she gave me fruit from the tree and I ate.' When God asks the woman about what has happened, she blames the serpent. This reminds me of a time when I was rebuking one of my children for some misdemeanor. 'The devil made me do it', he said by way of excuse.

In this profound story from Genesis we are reminded of our fatal tendency to lay blame, rather than accept responsibility for what we have done or failed to do. We lay the blame on others and get bitter toward them when things have gone wrong. At the end of this blame-line is God. A lot of people are angry with God. One way of punishing God is to stop believing in God. It's rather illogical when you think about it, but it's what we do.

Though Jesus makes it plain that there is no necessary connection between sin and sickness (see John 9:1-3), he doesn't rule it out. It's interesting that, in the case of the paralyzed man lowered through a hole in the roof by his friends, Jesus began the healing process by assuring him that his sins were forgiven. After that he told him to pick up his bed and walk (Mark 2:1-12).

When we are troubled, or sick, or angry and bitter, we do well to accept responsibility for our own part in it. Part of the process of being healed in body, mind and spirit is asking one another for forgiveness for the blame we've scattered around and dumped on others, including God. Jesus came to heal the enmity between people and to reconcile us to God. He wants us to be channels of his wholeness reconciled to God and one another—and to put aside our habit of blaming. *persecution complex*

For Thought and Discussion

1. Can you think of cases (perhaps even in your own life) when stopping the 'blame game' has been part of a person's growth toward healing?

2. Discovering forgiveness and re-establishing relationships is part of the work of healing. When have you found this to be true? *Deb . Diane*

3. How do we go about seeking inner healing? What sort of steps should we take?

3

Am I My Brother's or Sister's Keeper?

Readings: Genesis 4:1-10; Hebrews 12:14,15

As in the case of the Adam and Eve story, the story of their two sons—Cain and Abel and their falling out—is of universal application. Sin is always 'lurking at the door' of our lives and relationships, even the close ones. Jealousies and rivalries can easily arise in families, amongst friends, in and between churches, communities and nations. As the writer of the Letter to the Hebrews puts it, 'a root of bitterness' can easily get embedded in us and can subtly poison our attitudes and ways of relating to other people.

Abel was a pastoralist and Cain was an agriculturalist, giving a hint that the story is about tribal differences as well as the differences between two brothers. Abel's offering to the Lord (his worship) is accepted by God while Cain's is not. When Cain complains about this to God, the Lord reminds him that his worship needs to be pure—free from manipulation and backed up by righteous actions. There are always those who want to worship without dealing with what is wrong in their lives and what is unjust in the way they treat others. Jesus spoke of God seeking those who would worship 'in spirit and in truth'. Worshipping 'in truth' suggests that we need to take what is happening in our lives along with us when we worship. Jesus spoke of first being reconciled to our brother or sister before we offer our gift before the altar (see Matthew 5:21-24). He might well have had the Cain and Abel story in mind as he talked.

We are not competitors with one another in seeking God's attention, nor are we meant to be jealous of another's apparent favor with God. We are equally precious in God's sight and we do well to remember this as we draw near to God—that all human beings are brothers and sisters before the Lord.

It was certainly an extreme reaction on Cain's part to kill his brother through religious jealousy. Yet we are not unfamiliar with religious wars and terrible conflicts between people of different religious backgrounds. The third millennium certainly needs to be marked by religious toleration or human brothers and sisters will destroy one another over similar questions which faced Cain. 'Where is your brother?', says God. 'Am I my brother's keeper?' replies Cain. 'The voice of your brother's blood cries out to me from the ground' is God's word of judgment on Cain. Those words echo down the centuries and will continue to do so.

As we enter into healing ministry and prayer we believe that God is concerned about our diseases of the body. Jesus showed this; he healed people who came to him with all kinds of sickness—'they brought to him all the sick, those who were afflicted with various diseases and pains, demoniacs, epileptics, and paralytics, and he cured them' (Matthew 4:24,25). However, God is also concerned about our diseases of relationship—our resentments, angers, jealousies, carelessness of others and our hard-heartedness toward them. God demands of us a sense of responsibility for others—all of our brothers and sisters. Jesus understood this well, and told us that to be angry with our brother and sister was as bad as murdering them in the eyes of God (Matthew 5:21,22).

So we need to come in a spirit of repentance and a willingness to recognize the 'root of bitterness' that may be in our heart toward another or even toward God himself. Such poison in us may well be a cause of sickness or a barrier to healing taking place.

For Thought and Discussion

1. Are there any poisons of bitterness in me which I need to deal with? Are there any in my church? In my family? In my inherited attitudes?

2. Some physical illnesses are the body's reaction to an inner state of turmoil or distress in mind and heart. Can you think of examples of this?

3. Consider the promise of Isaiah 61:4: 'They shall build up the ancient ruins, they shall raise up the former devastations'. How might this promise apply to healing ministry and prayer?

4

None of These Diseases . . .

Readings: Deuteronomy 7:12-15, 28:58-61

The Book of Deuteronomy claims to be the words of Moses to the people of Israel after he has led them for forty years through the wilderness and they are about to enter the Promised Land. The book contains strong promises and warnings centering around Israel's need to be faithful to the one true God and not to lapse into the idolatry of the people of the land they were about to enter. They were not to forget the dependence upon God they had learned during their experience of deliverance from Egypt and their wilderness wanderings.

Moses set out the law of God for Israel based on the Ten Commandments (recorded for the second time in this book—Deuteronomy means 'the Second Book of the Law'). But Moses also exhorts Israel not to return to the kind of life they had known before. During their wanderings they had often hankered after Egypt, forgetting the worst aspects of life there, including the diseases they and their stock and their crops had suffered. During their wilderness experience, the people of God had discovered a freedom from disease. They had also discovered that God is a healer: 'I am the Lord who heals you' (see Exodus 15:22-27).

Thus embedded within the story and the faith of the people of God is a belief that God is a healer, and that God provides a healthy way of life for them. The law of God is a law of health and wholeness. Throughout the Hebrew Scriptures shalom (peace) is spoken of as a state of physical and spiritual well-being and blessing which is God's will for us. Our unfaithfulness or rebellion against God and the following of other 'gods' will open us up to disease and suffering. Deuteronomy warns that such rebellion will include a constant disquiet of mind and spirit: 'Your life shall hang in doubt before you; night and day you shall be in dread, with no assurance of your life. In the morning you shall say, 'If only it were evening!' and at evening you shall say, 'If only it were morning'—because of the dread your heart shall feel' (Deuteronomy 28:66,67).

These are terrible warnings. They suggest to us a strong connection between sin and sickness, between rebellion against God and disease. We may well protest that we have suffered from some sickness or disease or from psychological depression like what is described above without being in rebellion against God. The Book of Job deals with this basic question which all human beings ponder when confronted with innocent suffering. This long and remarkable poem certainly shows that the conventional approach— 'you are sick: you must have sinned'—is inadequate. Sin may cause sickness, but not all sickness is caused by sin.

Yet we have to admit that there is a lifestyle—a path of life— which God sets before us in the commandments and in the laws of health which he gives us. If we are Christians we add to this the importance of following Jesus' new commandment: 'Love one another as I have loved you'. Loving and forgiving contribute to a healthy lifestyle.

We have to admit, too, that there are sicknesses which are directly associated with sinful behavior and attitudes of mind. Over-indulgence in food, alcohol or drugs, laziness and lack of exercise (or the opposite: overwork and lack of proper rest and recreation), sexual promiscuity, ingrained hatreds or resentments—all these behaviors and attitudes can lead to sickness and disease of one kind or another.

Certainly the selfish and affluent lifestyle demanded by Western societies involves the exploitation of the earth's resources in an unjust and foolish way, insofar as they create wealth for the few but fail to address poverty, disease and lack of health care for the majority in the third world.

Where people suffer we complain of an unjust and cruel God, yet these are basically human problems which can be remedied by human beings. God wants us to be channels of his shalom and to be concerned not only for our own but also each other's health.

For Thought and Discussion

1. Think about and discuss the apparent difference of approach between Deuteronomy 28 and the Book of Job concerning the connection between sickness and sin. What has been your experience of the relationship?

2. How might we engage in 'preventive medicine' by attending to matters of lifestyle and faith?

3. Pray a prayer for God's shalom in the world and in us.

5

The Serpent on the Pole

Readings: Numbers 21:4-9, John 3:14-16

In the Numbers passage we have an account of an experience of healing while the people of God were on their wilderness journey. It's a strange story but it has great symbolic power. The serpent on the pole symbol has links through John's gospel with the cross of Jesus and its healing power. The symbol, you will note, is still used by the medical profession on its badges and banners.

Being bitten by poisonous snakes was one of the hazards of life in the wilderness. The people were in a state of rebellion and discontent against God and the leadership of Moses. Many of them died from snake bite and this was seen as a punishment from God. Moses was told to make a bronze serpent and set it on a pole; if the people looked upon it they would be cured. In a mysterious way this may be an early understanding of an antidote—the serpent itself provides the antidote for its poison. When we think of the cross—the lifting up of the Son of Man for all the world to see—a similar effect occurs. The antidote for sin is sin doing its worst against Jesus 'who became sin for us' (2 Corinthians 5:21).

There is a tradition in Christian teaching that Jesus Christ, in dying and rising again, not only won a victory over sin and death, but over sickness as well. This understanding goes right back into the Hebrew Scriptures and the prophecy of Isaiah concerning the Suffering Servant. 'Surely he has borne our infirmities and carried our diseases' (Isaiah 53:4). This text is certainly applied to Jesus by Matthew's gospel with direct reference to Jesus' healing ministry (see Matthew 8:16,17).

We look upon the cross of Jesus by faith. He was lifted up there for us, for our healing and salvation. When we pray for a sick person we may well think of Christ's finished work upon the cross that our wholeness may be restored. This gives us confidence to claim completeness of healing for the person which we believe Jesus has already accomplished in advance. This is strong stuff, but with God extreme remedies meet extreme need.

Salvation and healing are closely linked in the Bible. In the New Testament the words 'to save', 'to heal', 'to make whole' are different ways of translating the same word. 'Jesus saves' can also be rendered as 'Jesus heals'. Salvation can thus be seen a present experience—not just a future state.

Moses' snake on the pole reminds us of the poison of inner states of mind and heart which affect us as individuals or groups of people. The Letter to the Ephesians, one of the great pieces of writing in the New Testament, speaks of Jesus' death having literally 'killed the enmity' between Jews and Gentiles (Ephesians 2: 15). In other words Jesus wrought a great act of healing on the cross—reconciling us to God and to one another and, we could add, even to ourselves.

John's gospel speaks of Jesus being lifted up like the snake on the pole. Although it is clear that this is referring to Jesus' death when he was lifted up on the cross and also what this gospel calls his glorification (being exalted into God's eternal presence), there is a strong message to the Christian community, then and now, that Jesus is to be lifted up for all to see: 'But I, when I am lifted up from the earth, will draw all people to myself (John 12:32). These words were spoken at the time when some Greeks had come looking for Jesus. Jesus is to be the Savior and healer of people of all nations. It is our task to lift him up as a focus of faith for all kinds of people. Those who look on him and believe will find wholeness of being.

For Thought and Discussion

1. Healing is often more than a physical cure. What other kinds of healing do we need?

2. Reflect on how the serpent on the pole image can be made intelligible to people of today.

3. What are some of the ways we can 'lift Jesus up' for others to see?

6

Healing in the Psalms: God Hears Our Cry

Readings: Psalms 22, 42, 130

There is a great variety in the Psalms—the hymn book of the people of Israel. There are psalms of communal and personal praise, songs of thanksgiving for deliverance past and present, prayers for forgiveness and healing and cries of lament from the depths of human suffering. There seems to be a psalm to match almost every human mood—they can be our companions for life. They are songs for our pilgrimage.

The life of faith, and for that matter all human life, seems to consist of lots of ups and downs. There are times of despair, depression and darkness when God seems far off, as well as times of joy when we express spontaneous thanksgiving for the grace and help of God. The Psalms express this polarity, often within the one psalm. Psalm 22 is well known because the opening verse—according to Matthew and Mark—was part of Jesus' bitter and God-forsaken cry on the cross. This and the cry recorded by Luke, 'Father, into your hands I commend my spirit', which is a quote from Psalm 31, suggest to us that the words of the Psalms came readily to Jesus' lips. One can imagine him being sustained by words such as these. If you look at the experience of suffering, rejection and abuse described in Psalm 22 you can see that it is not far from Jesus' experience on the cross. If you read the whole psalm, you will see that there is a section of praise at the conclusion of the psalm and a significant change of mood. Some commentators claim that this section must have come from a different source. Yet it is this juxtaposition of desolation and moments of trust and praise which characterizes a number of the psalms. Perhaps there is significance in this juxtaposition and it reflects the paradoxical nature of human life and experience.

Psalm 42 seems to reflect the experience of an Israelite in exile—of a person cut off from the temple and its worship and surrounded by strange sounds and experiences. The taunt comes continually to the believer: 'Where now is your God?' Again it is not unlike the taunts to Jesus on the cross. When a series of bad things happen to us, we might well hear that question, or ask it ourselves. The psalmist is cast down in spirit and deeply depressed: 'Why have you forgotten me?' Yet in the midst of all the alienation and near-despair the believer cries out, 'Hope in God; for I shall again praise him, my help and my God.' If you read on to Psalm 43 you will see a very similar psalm with the cry of faith coming in as a kind of refrain. Repeated refrains often occur in hymns and psalms and express the need for cries of faith and confidence in God to be built into our lives. They can come to our rescue in times of need.

The classic cry from a point of deepest need is Psalm 130, sometimes referred to as the 'De Profundis' (from the first two words of the psalm in Latin). Our faith is that there is no point of human suffering and need lower than God will come to. He comes alongside us and to our aid at the bottom of the pit. The message of Christ's incarnation is that he emptied himself and took the lowest form, even the form and experience of a crucified slave, rejected by his people and cursed by the law of God in order to save us. It was no half measure; he didn't come half way down into the pit; he came right into the muck at the bottom to raise us up.

We see this in Jesus' healing ministry. He laid hands on a

leper, angry that the law forbade him to do so; he sat and talked as an equal with an adulterous Samaritan woman; he heard the desperate cry of a blind man in the crowd; he went into the graveyard to meet and heal a desperately disordered and violent man. We believe that Jesus' ministry to the outcast and needy and marginalized is a picture to us of the nature of God. It shows a God who hears the cries from the deepest and most desperate places of need and despair. Such a God is the God of the Psalms. Such a God is our God.

For Thought and Discussion

1. Recall (and perhaps share) moments of very deep need in your life or the life of someone near to you. In what ways did faith in God help or not help?

2. If you are in a group, share some verses from the Psalms which have helped you.

3. Discuss some of the juxtapositions of negative and positive experiences which you have experienced (say, in times of sickness).

7

Healing in the Psalms: Praise is Health-Giving

Readings: Psalms 67, 92, 150

The Psalms present us with the idea that it is a life-giving experience to praise God—on our own and with other people. 'It is good to give thanks to the Lord' is the plain opening statement of Psalm 92.

Just as deep breathing of fresh air and the full use of our lung capacity improves our state of health, so praise and a sense of wonder and exuberant thankfulness has a multiplying effect on our spiritual and physical health. The more we develop our capacity for praise, the more we can enjoy being alive. The great closing acclamation of the Book of Psalms is: 'Let everything that breathes praise the Lord! Praise the Lord!' The Hebrew expression 'Hallelujah' (Praise the Lord) has come into our language of praise.

Praise centers us on God, enabling our being to be part of the energy of creation. To the believer, 'the world is charged with the grandeur of God', as the poet Gerard Manley Hopkins puts it. We think of creation as uttering wordless praise, while we human beings, the priests of creation as it were, give words to our praise, and clap, dance and play musical instruments to give expression to it. The Psalms mention all these activities in connection with worship, and exhort all creatures and everything that lives and breathes to praise God. The heavenly bodies are included too: 'Praise him, sun and moon; praise him all you shining stars! Praise him you highest heavens, and you waters above the heavens!' (Psalm 148:3,4). Francis of Assisi, a true man of God, lived and expressed this kind of cosmic praise in his Canticle of the Sun, where Brother Sun and Sister Moon and all God's creatures are bidden to praise the Lord.

Being at one with the physical creation is an important part of health and wholeness. We live in a fourfold relationship—with God, with one another, with ourselves, and with the natural order. These harmonious relationships as planned by God are often broken—we lose our wholeness and need to be healed and reconciled in all four aspects of our living. We praise God because he binds up what is broken and makes us whole. As the hymn writer puts it, we are 'ransomed, healed, restored, forgiven'. So our hymns, psalms and spiritual songs are expressions of this reality. They are songs of health and salvation. Psalm 67 expresses strongly the connection between the praises of God and the blessing of health and prosperity.

Praise also joins us to one another. When we worship corporately and praise God together we experience a deep unity which cuts across all human divisions. We are united together under God and are called to practice justice toward one another: 'Let the nations be glad and sing for joy, for you judge the peoples with equity and guide the nations upon earth' (Psalm 67:4).

Note the expression 'peoples'—'let all the peoples praise you'. The psalm helps us to express our human solidarity that we are all brothers and sisters before God, despite our ethnic, national or religious differences.

The praises of God also lift us out of excessive self concern and enable us to be centered on God. They increase our sense of thankfulness and this in turn opens us up to receiving more blessing. We could say that the blessings of God are always there for us to draw on, but we are not always in the mood to receive them. In fact, we can be spiritually blind and deaf, and hardly notice the gifts and opportunities which God puts before us.

The wonderful thing about praise is that it opens us up to God, like flowers opening to the sun. We could carry the same image through to an understanding of healing—we need to be opened up to the healing light of God and to the healing energy of God's spirit being stirred within us.

For Thought and Discussion

1. Recall great moments of praise in your life. Was there a health-giving element in these moments? How was it manifested?

2. The Psalms (e.g., Psalms 92, 119:164) speak of praising God at different times of the day. What does this suggest to us?

3. What is praise like in your local church? Can you suggest ways of building up healthy praise?

8

A Foreigner Gets Cured

Reading: 2 Kings 5: 1-14

There are a number of examples of the prophets of the Hebrew Scriptures having a ministry of healing. The prophets brought God's word to their nation at times when they had wandered from God and were slipping into idolatry. Often people asked for blessings from gods 'that were no gods' and followed all kinds of detestable practices which dishonored and hurt their human dignity. They needed to seek again the true God to find their wholeness and follow the laws of communal and personal health given them by the one true God, the 'I am who I am.'

About eight centuries before Christ, Elijah and his disciple Elisha performed miracles of healing in God's name. As recounted in the First and Second Book of Kings, people who were not of the nation of Israel heard of the work of these men of God and their powerful witness to the Lord of all. Naaman, the general of the Aramean army, suffered from leprosy and heard of Elisha, the man of God in Israel, from a servant girl in Naaman's wife's household. She said: 'If only my lord were with the prophet who is in Samaria! He would cure him of his leprosy.'

When Naaman came to Elisha he told him to go and wash seven times in the River Jordan. As you would have read in this beautifully told story, Naaman was cranky and intensely disappointed: 'I thought that he would surely come out, and stand and call on the name of the Lord his God, and would wave his hand over the spot and cure the leprosy.' He wanted spectacular signs and impressive ceremonies to match his standing and importance. However, his servants encouraged him to do what he had been told to do and Naaman humbled himself and went and washed himself seven times in this seemingly insignificant river. Naaman was healed of his leprosy and he went away thankful and believing.

There are a number of lessons we could learn from this story:

1. *'Outsiders' have access to the grace and healing power of God.* Naaman was the military general of the Arameans, a nation which often was a threat to Israel. He was one of the enemy. Through his healing Naaman came to know that there is no God in all the earth except in Israel (1 Kings 5:15). This God is not confined in his working and his care to any nation. The Christian faith strongly declares that God 'shows no partiality' (see Acts 10:35) and there are no 'outsiders' with God. We do well to mind our prejudices.

2. *We often need to be humbled to receive God's help.* God doesn't do things in the way that we expect. Naaman's natural and national pride had to be quelled for him to be able to dip himself seven times in a river he thought far inferior to the rivers of his own country. He had to put his prejudices aside. Elisha didn't even come out of his house to meet this important person—he sent a messenger to tell him to wash in the Jordan seven times. Naaman initially expected more honorific treatment. Those used to ordering others about and taking leadership (even in ministry) have to put themselves into the position of being humble receivers.

3. *We need to surrender ourselves completely in faith to the full healing process.* Naaman needed to complete seven different immersions in the Jordan. In Hebrew seven is the complete number—it suggests going right through with something.

Naaman must have felt a fool in the middle of the pro-cess—'surely four times is enough!' But he did what he was told to do, and he did it properly and thoroughly. Is there a lesson here about obedience and faith?

For Thought and Discussion

1. Describe any occasions when you or your church com-munity have slipped into prejudiced attitudes toward oth-ers and thought of them as beyond the reach of God's care and grace.

2. Think about and discuss the difficulties we sometimes have in being 'humble receivers.' Why do we have these difficulties?

3. Do we have too narrow a concept of how healing min-istry should take place? Can you describe some unusual means of healing in the Scriptures or in your own experi-ence?

9

A Fig Poultice

Reading: Isaiah 38

I have vivid memories of a mustard poultice being applied to my chest when I was a child suffering from bronchitis. In my mother's family this was a traditional remedy for bad chests. In Hezekiah's sickness, Isaiah tells him to apply a traditional remedy, and Hezekiah recovers.

We do not know what kind of sickness King Hezekiah was suffering from; some commentators think it was the plague, and that the appearance of the boil was a hopeful sign. The application of a bunch of figs to help draw the infection was apparently a common traditional remedy. The biblical story reminds us that God provides medicinal and pharmaceutical substances for us as part of the created order. Lighting upon the right substance to use in particular cases is part of the practical wisdom which has been handed down from the experience of the past. Modern methods of research help us to have confidence in this or that medicinal remedy. We do well to take the medicines prescribed for us in our times of sickness.

In the roll of good kings and bad kings of Israel and Judah in 1 and 2 Kings and 1 and 2 Chronicles, Hezekiah comes up as one of the good ones. Hezekiah ruled in Jerusalem not long before its conquest by Babylon and he turned the people back to the worship of God. He got rid of the idolatrous practices which the people of Jerusalem were following; and, at the time when the Assyrians besieged Jerusalem, Hezekiah turned to God and the advice of the prophet Isaiah. Miraculously the enemy turned about and left, because of the rumor of troubles elsewhere. All this is dramatically told in Isaiah chapters 36 and 37 and likewise almost parallel passages in 2 Kings 18 and 19. When Hezekiah fell ill he called for the prophet Isaiah who told him that he was going to die. Hezekiah turned his face to the wall, wept bitterly and cried out to the Lord, asking him to remember how he had sought to please God. Isaiah then passed on a message from God that Hezekiah's prayer was heard, and that he would recover and have a further fifteen years added to his life.

According to Isaiah 38:9-20, we have a detail of Hezekiah's prayer, which he wrote down subsequently. It is a deep cry from the heart for healing: 'Oh restore me to health and make me live!' Hezekiah says of his experience of sickness: 'Surely it was for my welfare that I had great bitterness'. Often we come out of a time of sickness and desperate need with a greater sense of dependence on God and a deeper thankfulness (see Isaiah 38: 17-20).

These accounts present us with an understanding that God is responsive to prayer and that he hears genuine cries for help. There are some theological questions which believers and intercessors have to face. Why pray if God already knows our need? Does God change his mind as a result of our prayers? How does intercessory prayer work? Unquestionably God knows our need. It is apparently not part of God's nature to exercise control over everything that we do, but to give us a certain independence and ability to make our own choices. Without this freedom to choose there could be no growth to maturity on our part and no genuine loving, no heroic decisions, no problem-solving on our part, no reaching out to one another in our times of need or uncertainty—it would all be done for us. Any wise parent understands these dynamics in the bringing up of children—too much control is not healthy. So the omnipotent God accepts limitations and the possibility that things may go badly wrong in order that we may have our own part to play in the healing process and our growth to maturity.

God chooses to give a place to asking prayer. We can ask for help for ourselves and others. Jesus encouraged us to do this: 'Ask and it will be given to you, seek and you will find; knock and the door will be opened for you.' Hezekiah, in his deepest need, asked for his life to be spared and God heard the prayer from a believing and repentant heart and healed him (with the fig poultice playing its part).

For Thought and Discussion

1. What dynamics do you think are happening when we engage in prayer for healing?

2. Can you think of modern medicines which have their source in traditional folk remedies?

3. What part does God give us in the work of healing?

10

From the Belly of the Fish

Reading: The Book of Jonah (entire)

Consideration of the meaning of the Book of Jonah—one of the truly remarkable books of the Bible—is unfortunately bedeviled by arguments about whether someone can survive in the belly of a large fish for three days. It's an old parable story—a cautionary tale—about a Jewish man who refused initially to go to Nineveh, a large and godless city, to proclaim God's word, and his resentment when God forgives the Ninevites and shows mercy on them.

In the latter part of the story it is revealed that the reason for Jonah's initial disobedience to God is that he knew God would show mercy on Nineveh and he didn't want that. He wanted them to have their come-uppances! When Jonah turned against God's call to be a missionary to Nineveh he went off in exactly the opposite direction and took a boat to Tarshish. Jonah was certainly aware of what he was doing and his own willful disobedience. When the storm came and the ship began to break up the sailors realized that there were terrible consequences to Jonah's disobedience. They knew his story 'because he had told them so'. 'Pick me up and throw me into the sea', was Jonah's advice. They took it.

From inside the belly of the fish which God had appointed to swallow Jonah, he prayed to the Lord. The prayer begins with a realization of his deep distress; yet he trusts that the Lord hears him and will save him. There is a very good description of the dark side of human experience and the depressed states we can get into: 'I went down to the land whose bars closed upon me forever'. The land 'whose bars closed upon me' may also refer to the terrible time of exile which the Jewish people suffered in Babylon. They came to understand this to be a result of their disobedience to God and lack of missionary vision.

At the deepest point of need, when 'his life was ebbing away', Jonah remembered the Lord; his prayer came before God; the Lord spoke to the fish and it vomited Jonah out onto dry land. Jonah then decides that obedience is the better course. Jonah goes to Nineveh and proclaims the message to them 'according to the word of the Lord'. The Ninevites repent and are forgiven by God; yet Jonah, rather than being pleased, is angry. It's apparently not the first time that he has remonstrated with God about his propensity to forgive sinners; now he is almost suicidal in his anger. God asks Jonah whether his anger is really justified, but Jonah still in a huff goes out into the heat, makes a booth and sits there in the heat of the day and in the heat of his own anger.

God in his mercy provides a tree to shade Jonah and Jonah is grateful. God then causes the tree to wither, and Jonah is in a bad way. He still wants to die. He utters a cry the opposite of the usual prophet's message. It is the ultimate statement of despair—'It is better to die than live.'

God then says a very simple thing: 'You were sorry about the tree that died, shouldn't I be sorry for the people of Nineveh who were in danger of perishing without knowing me?' We are not told of Jonah's response. The story reminds us of Jesus' attempts to speak to the righteous people of his own time (represented by the angry elder brother in the parable of the Prodigal Son, or by those who have borne the burden and heat of the day in the parable of the laborers in the market place) 'Are you envious because I am generous?' (Matthew 20: 15).

There are strong lessons here for us when we undergo times of sickness which can turn out to be times of deep personal insight for us. Anger and resentment are often present. Why is this happening to me and not to those people who sin and yet seem to get off scot free? We may be going in wrong directions and need to reassess our lives and priorities. We can cry out to God from the depth of our need and we can admit our extreme anger to God. This is often a necessary preliminary step to our healing and restoration.

For Thought and Discussion

1. Think of (and perhaps share) times of adversity in your life which have been major points of growth in self-understanding or understanding of God's mercy.

2. Underline or mark points of recognition in the Jonah story—points where you recognize yourself, your own experience or the experience of others. Share these in discussion.

3. How did God help Jonah recognize his anger and resentment and deal with his depression?

11

A Healing Manifesto

Readings: Isaiah 61:1-7, Luke 4:16-30

In the second part of the Book of Isaiah we have a number of prophecies which bring the good news of imminent deliverance for the people of God who have been in exile in Babylon. The prophet has a strong sense of personal call—an anointing from God—to bring healing deliverance and liberation to those in exile. They are to be delivered out of their prison, have their broken spirits healed and revived and given a garment of praise in place of their garments of servitude and bondage. The 'day' or time of the Lord's favor is going to be experienced.

Jesus took these words, read them to the congregation in the synagogue at Nazareth where he had grown up, and applied them to himself. In the record of Jesus' ministry in the gospels, we see that the words of Isaiah 61 were quite literally fulfilled. Jesus didn't bring a political deliverance as many of his followers hoped, but he did bring healing and deliverance and a new spiritual freedom to the poor, the oppressed, the sick and diseased, not only of his own nation—'the lost sheep of the house of Israel'—but to Samaritans and Gentiles as well.

These words from Isaiah 61 have become a kind of manifesto of healing and wholeness, spiritual and physical. God uses those who believe in him and his liberating power as agents of his healing. He continues to anoint us for the work of healing in the name of Jesus and the power of the Holy Spirit. Jesus came to be known as the Christ—the anointed one of God—by both his words and his deeds of power.

We may notice a significant difference between the over-all context of Isaiah 61 and that of Luke 4. In Isaiah 61 the Gentiles are to come and serve the people of Israel. In Luke 4, Jesus speaks of God's purpose to heal the Gentiles and outsiders and affirms here and elsewhere the universal character of his mission.

Confronted with this message of God's love to the whole world—not just to the tribe or nation—the local townspeople are offended. They are already angry with him because he hasn't done sufficient healings and miracles in his own home town. They turn against him and take him up to one of the local cliffs to toss him over, but Jesus calmly walks through the midst of them and goes on his way to do healing in other places. Mark tells us that Jesus could do few healings in his own home town and amongst his own people, 'being amazed at their unbelief' (see Mark 6: 1-6).

So we need God's anointing in order to be channels of his healing and liberating work. But we also need God's anointing in order to build up great communities of faith, communities with a large enough heart to respond to the breadth of his mission as made plain in the ministry, teach-ing and healing work of Jesus, the anointed one of God.

Isaiah's healing and liberating manifesto will no doubt continue to inspire specific ministries of hope and healing on the part of the servants of God, but within the wide and all-embracing context of Jesus' mission to the whole world rather than what appears to be the narrower nationalistic vision of Isaiah 61.

For Thought and Discussion

1. Do you find the words of Isaiah 61:1-4 powerful? If so, why?

2. Reflect on how the ministry of Jesus and the healing ministry of the church fulfills the Isaiah verses.

3. How can we be sure that Jesus' broad vision of ministry is fulfilled in today's church?

12

Wisdom From an Earlier Jesus

Reading: Sirach 38:1-15 (from the Apocrypha)

Jesus, the son of Sirach, tells us that God created the physician and the pharmacist for our health. This Jesus says: 'The Lord created medicines out of the earth, and the sensible will not despise them' (38:4). When we are sick, we should certainly not neglect to seek out physicians, nurses, pharmacists, and other health professionals and to follow their advice—as 'their gift of healing comes from the Most High' (38:2).

There is a tendency in some Christian healing circles to seek healing only through faith, and to turn aside from the advice and help of medical professionals. Some who have felt in a healing service that they have been healed have then thrown away their medication or cancelled their appointment to see the doctor. This is not wise and has, at times, led to disastrous results.

This is not to say that people may not be instantly and miraculously healed after healing prayer and the exercise of faith. Some are set on the path to healing over a period of time, and the healing ministry experience has provided an important turn-around for them. However, just as Jesus of Nazareth sent the lepers off to the priests to have their healing certified, so if we feel that we have been healed we need to have the healing certified by an authorized person. If a true healing has taken place then that should become evident. We should not go off our medication, or reject medical advice lightly.

It is well to be aware that God works through those he creates and to whom he gives special skills, gifts and insights
to help bring about healing. We see the work of doctors,
pharmacists, paramedics and medical researchers as being
part of God's provision for us and we praise God for them.
To have faith in God for healing does not necessarily mean
that we turn away from medical advice and help. Rather
we pray that we will receive the right advice and help and
that God will guide those who have the care of us.

You will notice that the reading from Sirach assumes that
the physician will pray to God for a correct diagnosis.
Many doctors do just that. God is not limited in his use of
those who don't have specific belief—the Bible has a broad
view in this respect. Though we might be pleased to go to a
doctor who is a believer, it's best to choose the one with the
greatest skill, experience and understanding in the area in
which we need help. That doctor or specialist may indeed
be God's gift to us—God's answer to our prayer of faith.

Jesus son of Sirach includes some other important advice
for the sick. He says that we should not only pray to the
Lord for healing, but that we should amend our lives and
cleanse our hearts from all sin. As we have noted elsewhere in these studies, there is no necessary connection
between sickness and sin in the direct causal sense, but
there may be some important change to our lifestyle or
to our attitudes of mind which is needful before we can
proceed to full health. Resentment against others, or guilt
over something for which we've never sought forgiveness,
can be barriers in us, blocking the way to healing. You will
recall that Jesus began his ministry to the paralyzed man
lowered down in front of him by assuring him of forgiveness (see Mark 2:1-12).

For Thought and Discussion

1. Reflect on the blessings brought to us by medical science. Why is there some unwillingness of the part of some believers to see this as part of the work of God?

2. Discuss the ways in which the church (or your group) could affirm the ministry of those who work in the medical, nursing and allied health professions.

3. How can repentance, confession and the assurance of forgiveness help us on the path to healing?

13

First Days of Jesus' Ministry

Reading: Mark 1:16-39

A characteristic of St Mark's gospel is the dramatic way in which we are plunged into the story. A rapid and exciting pace is sustained in this, the shortest of the four gospels. A favorite word of the author is translated as 'immediately', 'at once', or 'just then.' Most scholars believe it is the oldest of the four gospels and takes us closest to the oral traditions and stories of the first disciples.

According to Mark 1, soon after Jesus' baptism and his temptation time in the wilderness (very briefly described), Jesus calls his first disciples and begins a healing and deliverance ministry in Capernaum, the main trading town of Galilee. On the sabbath in the synagogue in Capernaum, Jesus delivers a man from possession with an evil spirit. The people notice a strong note of authority in Jesus' teaching and ministry and his fame begins to spread quickly in Galilee.

That same day Jesus went to Simon Peter's house, where he was staying. There he healed Peter's mother-in-law of a fever, taking her by the hand and lifting her up. That evening at sunset when the sabbath was over, many sick people were brought to Peter's house and much healing and deliverance ministry took place. Luke, in his account of the event, tells that Jesus laid hands on every one of the sick who was brought to him. He gave them individual attention (see Luke 4:38-41).

Mark comments that Jesus wouldn't allow the demons in

people to speak 'because they knew him'. Earlier in the day the man in the synagogue had started shouting out: 'What have you to do with us, Jesus of Nazareth? Have you come to destroy us? I know who you are, the Holy One of God.'

Jesus silenced the demonic spirit and commanded it to come out of the man. It is noteworthy that the spirits were the first to recognize Jesus for who he was, and sensed that in him they had more than met their match. In the presence of Jesus there is a confrontation with rebellious powers; we can take authority over them in Jesus' name and with the authority he gives to those who believe in him. Mark tells us that when Jesus commissioned the twelve disciples 'he gave them authority over the unclean spirits' and to heal the sick (see Mark 6:7-13). We can proceed with healing and deliverance ministry today in the name of Jesus and with the authority he gives us.

However we notice that Jesus didn't seek to be over-dramatic about healing and deliverance ministries, and he actively discouraged those who had been healed from talking about him and making him known. He certainly didn't welcome the publicity being given him by the evil spirits.

Mark's gospel has sometimes been called the 'Gospel of the Messianic Secret'. This aspect of the gospel may puzzle us. Perhaps there was so much misunderstanding about what the Messiah would do that he took care not to seek excessive publicity. It is clear that he was tempted to be a sign-giving Messiah, and for various reasons avoided stepping centrally into that role. He clearly wanted to lead people into deeper things in their relationship with God, and didn't want to leave them only on the fringes of that relationship. It is also clear from the gospel records that he introduced people to the harder, more challenging parts of what it meant to be his disciples as they traveled along with him, rather than revealing everything at once.

In relation to the healing ministry and its practice today, there may be some important insights to gain from observing and reflecting on Jesus' ministry. Is physical healing an end in itself? Is there a danger in making 'signs and wonders' a main plank in the church's platform? Is there a certain amount of confidentiality and discreetness needed around the ministry of healing? Would we do well to heed Jesus' example of withdrawal for prayer and solitude after being engaged in heavy ministry, as described by Mark in 1:35?

For Thought and Discussion

1. Give attention to the questions of the last paragraph of this study.

2. There may be some apprehensions about deliverance ministry and talk of dealing with 'unclean spirits'. How appropriate is this ministry in the contemporary world?

3. Think about and discuss the place of a sense of authority in ministry, and healthy and unhealthy manifestations of authority.

14

Confrontation and Healing

Readings: Mark 3:1-6, Matthew 12:9-14

Here we have almost parallel accounts of the same healing, but each account highlights in a slightly different way the dramatic clash between Jesus and those who accused him of breaking the sabbath law by healing on the sabbath.

It was in the synagogue (at Capernaum?) that Jesus saw a man with a withered hand. We are told that 'they watched him to see whether he would cure him on the sabbath so that they might accuse him'. Jesus' ministry was constantly under criticism. A carping, critical spirit can often take over religious people, so that they are quicker to criticize than to praise, more ready to condemn than show mercy or encourage. Lord defend us from such attitudes!

Jesus was deeply irritated by these negative attitudes. Mark tells us that Jesus called the man out to the front and looked around at his critics in anger, 'grieved by their hardness of heart.'

Matthew's account, though it doesn't specifically mention Jesus' anger, has an atmosphere of anger in what Jesus says to those watching in critical silence. 'Suppose one of you has only one sheep and it falls into a pit on the sabbath; will you not lay hold of it and lift it out? How much more valuable is a human being than a sheep?' After telling the man to stretch out his hand, the man does so in an act of faith in Jesus, and his hand is restored, with Matthew adding 'as sound as the other hand.' Under Jesus' ministry the man becomes a fully functioning human being.

All four gospels present to us a Jesus who is fully in touch with his own humanity. 'Gentle Jesus meek and mild' is hardly an apt description. He didn't hesitate to show his anger and his grieving spirit to those who offended his sense of compassion.

We do well to remember that Jesus often stirred up the religious elite and that he was eventually put to death because of his confrontation with them. Good church people sometimes do some awful things to others who differ from them. History is littered with examples of religious bigotry and narrow-mindedness.

Jesus treated the sabbath, which he saw as a gift from God for our health, as an ideal day in which to do works of restoration and healing. He looked for opportunities on the sabbath to bring God's love and healing to those who felt powerless, or who saw themselves as outsiders. His healing ministry always seems to have a note of challenge about it. What do you think about this aspect of ministry? Where do you stand?

It is a sad thing that many in the Christian church see the healing ministry as dangerous for the church and therefore refuse to move into it. Instead of the hand of healing power in God's name, there is often a withered, powerless hand.

Sometimes church authorities have sought to control and limit the healing ministry and to make their church 'non-controversial' in respect to various gifts of the Spirit and healing and deliverance ministries. Jesus' challenge to the man to stretch out his hand may sound a note of challenge to the church—'stretch out your hand to heal and bless.'

For Thought and Discussion

1. What challenges have come to you as you have studied the healing of the man with the withered hand?

2. Why is a sense of Jesus' humanity important in the way we present him?

3. Is your church and congregation comfortable with the exercise of healing ministry? How can this ministry be encouraged?

15

Teaching and Healing in Matthew

Reading: Matthew 4:23 - 5:12

Though we are familiar with Bibles which have chapters and verses marked to help us find our way about, we should remember that books of the Bible were originally written without chapter divisions and without numbered verses. So when we read them we should realize that there is often a natural flow-on from one chapter to the next.

In the reading set for this study we have a case in point. Chapter 4 of Matthew's gospel concludes with a description of all the people who came from all the regions around Galilee bringing with them people with all kinds of sicknesses, diseases of mind and body. Matthew says that Jesus cured 'every kind of disease and every sickness among the people'. As a result his fame spread like wildfire and large crowds followed him wherever he went.

Chapter 5 of the Gospel then tells us that when Jesus saw the crowds he went up a hill or mountain and sat down where it was convenient to speak to large numbers where they could see and hear him. He then taught them many things. We have in the following three chapters what we usually call 'The Sermon on the Mount.'

We notice as we read the gospels that there is double emphasis—on word and deed, on teaching and healing. One accompanies the other. You will find as you look at Matthew that there are a number of short passages inserted into the narrative where the author reminds us of the very extensive healing ministry of Jesus going on throughout his ministry. Matthew stresses very strongly the enormity of human need and Jesus' deep compassion for people. 'When he saw the crowds, he had compassion for them, because they were harassed and helpless, like sheep without a shepherd' (Matthew 9:56).

Many people with their whole range of needs sought out Jesus. He attended to their cries for help, and his healing sessions must have been long, dramatic and exhausting. No wonder Jesus took a number of opportunities to go away to quiet places for prayer and rest. He knew the importance of keeping a balance in his life. You will see that Jesus was insistent on teaching and making disciples. He was not merely a healer and wonder-worker. He introduced people to the secrets of the Kingdom of God. He told many parables—simple stories with deep spiritual truths—and gave many vivid and earthy illustrations of what it means to be servants of God and seekers after righteousness.

In Jesus we have a strong mix of challenging teaching and profound ministry, the like of which the world had not seen before and has not seen since. Jesus did, moreover, commission his followers to proclaim the kingdom of God and to heal the sick. It seems clear from the Gospels that we are to keep a balance between proclamation and healing as he did. One ministry complements the other.

When you think about it, we wouldn't think of omitting the proclamation and preaching side of our response to Jesus' commission to his followers; why then would we ignore the healing side to that commission? Two arms are better than one. It seems clear that Jesus wants us to face the world with two arms—the arm of proclamation and the arm of healing.

For Thought and Discussion

1. In what ways does your church keep (or fail to keep) the balance mentioned here between teaching and healing?

2. The Gospel of Matthew is at pains to point to the breadth of Jesus' healing ministry—'every kind of disease and every sickness among the people'. How can we take care to maintain this breadth in the church's life and ministry?

3. Are there some diseases or conditions that we regard as 'beyond the pale'—beyond the reach of God's healing power? Discuss.

16

Laid at Jesus' Feet

Reading: Mark 2:1-12

Those of us who went to Sunday School or church when we were children probably remember this story vividly: how four friends brought their paralyzed friend to Jesus. They were so determined to get him close to Jesus, but the crowd in and around the house was so great that they had to remove tiles and dig through the roof above, and lowered their friend down on his mat. It certainly is a memorable story showing how strong their faith and their love for their friend was.

The gospel account then says: 'When Jesus saw their faith he said to the paralytic, "Son, your sins are forgiven."' In Jesus' healing ministry we are told, in a number of cases, that he responded to the faith of those who brought others to him or made strong requests on their behalf. We are encouraged by this as we pray for our friends and relatives, bringing them, in faith, to Jesus' feet. Just as these four men combined their physical strength and ingenuity to bring their friend to Jesus, so their combined faith was also effective. To pray together for someone, in agreed faith, is like their combined action for their friend.

Jesus' first initiative with the paralyzed man is worth comment. He assured this man of the forgiveness of his sins. Matthew's account of the same episode has Jesus saying: 'Take heart, your sins are forgiven.' It seems that Jesus perceived that the man's deepest need was to be assured of his acceptance and forgiveness by God. Was he paralyzed by his own guilt? We do not know, but we do know that disturbed states of mind can lead to effects in the body, mind, spirit, and all are interconnected. Jesus' claim to be able to forgive sins caused muttering in the crowd concerning blasphemy. Who can forgive sins but God? Jesus, however, was quite comfortable about exercising this authority, and he demonstrated its power and effectiveness by telling the man to pick up his mat and walk.

Once again Jesus' ministry strikes a strong note of challenge and confrontation. His observers were challenged by his ministry of forgiveness and healing. The paralyzed man was also strongly challenged. Did he believe Jesus' word of forgiveness and healing?

Mark captures very powerfully the atmosphere: 'Jesus said to the paralytic: "I say to you, stand up, take up your mat and go to your home." And he stood up, and immediately took the mat and went out before all of them; so that they were all amazed . . .'

This passage raises some confronting questions for us. Is there a paralysis caused by unforgiven sin in our lives? Do we believe Jesus' word of forgiveness for ourselves or only for others? What are our deepest needs for healing? Can we make an immediate response to Jesus' presence and word as the paralyzed man did?

We also might well be stirred up by the action of the man's four friends. We often engage in intercessory prayer only half-heartedly and sometimes without seeking strong agreement from others. These four friends' agreed faith and persistence was certainly rewarded. It is a challenge to us to pray in a concerted and persevering way for those in need. It may help to picture our action as bringing our friends, through all barriers and discouragements, right to Jesus' feet.

For Thought and Discussion

1. Here Jesus makes a strong link between the man's forgiveness and healing. Is this always the case in Jesus' ministry? Discuss how forgiveness helps in the healing process.

2. Do you think that we are often slow to accept forgiveness for ourselves? Why is this so?

3. How can we become more effective in our prayer and action for others?

17

A Daughter of Abraham

Reading: Luke 13:10-17

St Luke records this healing of a woman who had been crippled for eighteen years. She was bent over and couldn't stand up straight. Jesus told her she was set free from her ailment and laid hands on her. Immediately she stood up straight and began praising God. It was a clear sign to all that Jesus was able to lift the burden of sickness from people—even long-standing sickness and infirmity.

Jesus did this healing in a synagogue on the sabbath day, and the leader of the synagogue rebuked Jesus for healing on the sabbath. People should come on the other six days to be healed and not on the sabbath day. This was one of many such occasions when Jesus was thus rebuked.

Jesus was not soft in his reply, calling his critics hypocrites for not hesitating to release their ox or donkey from its stall to water it on the sabbath, and not rejoicing that this woman was liberated from her bondage to this illness on the sabbath. He refers to the woman as 'a daughter of Abraham'. She is not only physically healed but she is restored to her full dignity as a daughter of Abraham and member of the people of God.

It is clear that Jesus had a special care for the marginalized and those who were easily overlooked. He had a ministry with women, who were not always accorded their full dignity as human beings in the society in which he moved. Those Jewish men who enjoyed the benefits of their religion through the proud title 'sons of Abraham' would have

noticed the pointed way in which Jesus called this former-
ly crippled woman 'a daughter of Abraham.' Part of the
burden of her sickness would have been the sense of being
cursed by God and punished for her or her family's sin. In
her healing she is set free in more ways than one.

For those who knew their Bible, there would be powerful
religious symbolism in setting someone free on the sabbath. In the Deuteronomic version of the Ten Commandments, the reason for keeping the sabbath, when the male
and female slaves are given a day of rest as well as those of
the household, is that they were to remember that they had
been slaves in the land of Egypt. 'Therefore the Lord your
God commanded you to keep the sabbath day' (Deuteronomy 5:15). How appropriate then that the sabbath should
be used to liberate someone who has been bound for eighteen years!

In the ministry Jesus gives us to be channels of healing in
his name, there is always the dimension of setting people
free. As noted before, Jesus sees his ministry as fulfilling
the vision of Isaiah 61 where the anointed one sets the cap-
tives free, and gives them a garment of praise instead of a
spirit of heaviness. Surely that is our ministry in the spirit
and tradition of Jesus Christ.

We are called to accord people their full dignity. Jesus never
condescended or 'ministered down' to people. He saw their
need for acceptance and affirmation and encouraged them
to stand up straight as sons and daughters of God. Let us
take care that in all our ministries of care and healing we
maintain a constant attitude of treating people, whoever
they are, no matter what their background or disablement,
with the full dignity due to them. We are to be watchful
against any treatment of human beings which demeans or
diminishes them in the eyes of others.

For Thought and Discussion

1. Think of other episodes in Jesus' ministry where Jesus treats women despised by others with dignity. Has the church been true to the Jesus tradition in this respect?

2. Sickness and disability often have an alienating and isolating effect. How can we be used to counteract this?

3. In what specific ways should we work to protect human dignity in ministries of healing?

18

'What do you want me to do for you?'

Reading: Mark 10:46-52

Jesus' question to the blind man Bartimaeus seems almost superfluous. Surely it was obvious that Bartimaeus would want to get his sight back. Jesus apparently wanted him to make the request for himself. There is a frequent reference in the New Testament to asking: 'Ask and you shall receive.' James' Epistle makes the point that we often do not receive because we do not ask (see James 4:2).

It is good for us to make requests to God or to another person for our needs. Asking outloud clarifies in our own mind as to what we really are seeking; it stretches our faith to do the asking for ourselves; it helps us to forsake our typical independent stance—'I can manage very well on my own, thank you.'

Jesus also seems to be teaching us that in ministering to others the focus should be on the real need of the person being ministered to—that is, *really* listening to their needs and not making assumptions. Sometimes in our urgent need to be of help we rush in and overdo the helping, almost smothering the person with 'our' ministry. This was not Jesus' way.

The Bartimaeus story is illuminating in other ways too. The blind man was part of a large crowd mobbing Jesus and his disciples as they left Jericho. He kept calling out: 'Jesus, Son of David, have mercy on me.' Others in the crowd ordered Bartimaeus to be quiet. Who did this blind beggar think he was, making all this racket? Why would he claim Jesus' attention, when there were plenty of more worthy people needing to hear and see him?

The account of Bartimaeus' healing, as so often in Mark's gospel, is very dramatic. 'Jesus stood still and said "Call him here".' Jesus heard the cry of Bartimaeus from the edge of the large crowd which was surrounding him. Many might be calling out, but the Lord hears the individual cry of need and prayer of faith. It stretches our faith to believe that in the midst of all the world's need and the millions of prayers which must come to God's ears that he will hear *my* cry and recognize *my* need. Some people refrain from praying about their own needs at all, saying something like: 'I'm not important enough, my need is not great when I compare myself with all the other needy and deprived people of the world.' Jesus would encourage us otherwise. As one of our healing ministry songs says: 'He will hear your faintest cry'.

The Orthodox churches teach their members to pray the 'Jesus Prayer': 'Lord Jesus Christ, Son of God, have mercy on me'. They are taught to repeat this prayer many times, until it becomes as natural as breathing. It keeps us in a constant state of faith and dependence on Jesus, who is always with us, as he promised. The prayer reminds us of Bartimaeus' cry from the crowd. Each individual person is important to the God of the whole universe. Jesus wants us to know that.

When Bartimaeus came to Jesus and made his request: 'My teacher, let me see again', the text tells us that he used the expression 'Rabbouni', the Aramaic word used by Mary Magdalene when she greeted the risen Jesus in the garden on Easter morning. It was a moment of recognition and joyful faith for her. For Bartimaeus, this chance meeting with Jesus was certainly a life-changing experience. We are told by Mark: 'Immediately he regained his sight and followed him on the way'. So Bartimaeus was not only healed of his blindness; he became a disciple of Jesus.

For Thought and Discussion

1. Reflect on the changes that would have taken place in Bartimaeus' life and attitudes following this day in Jericho. Are there any parallels in your life?

2. What insights have you gained from the Bartimaeus passage about (a) your own prayer life? (b) your ministry to others?

3. Is the constant use of the 'Jesus Prayer', or some equivalent, something that is, or would be, helpful for you?

19

'Do you want to be healed?'

Reading: John 5:1-18

Jesus' question 'Do you want to be healed?' is a searching and challenging one. The man lying by the pool had been there (or at least brought there every day) for thirty-eight years. Whenever the water in the pool is disturbed—supposedly by an angel representing God's presence—he says he is unable to get there first. The tradition was that whoever got into the pool first after such a disturbance in the water would be healed. Now, thirty-eight years is a very long time to be paralyzed. After awhile a chronically sick person's disease may become part of their identity, their pre-occupation, and even their occupation. The sickness may become the basis for their livelihood—in former times by begging, today through a sickness benefit or compensation. The paralyzed man's answer to Jesus' question shows that he has a well-polished explanation for his plight.

John recounts that Jesus spoke firmly to the man, telling him to stand up, take up his mat and walk. At once the man was healed, took up his mat and began to walk. Faith was strongly stirred in him by Jesus. He was prepared to be a changed and healed person with all that that involved for his life. We not only admire Jesus for the works of healing he did, giving powerful signs of God's presence in the world; we admire the paralyzed man for having the courage to be a different person without his usual props.

It is infuriatingly negative and nitpicking of some of the Jewish leaders to not rejoice in this man's healing and instead to criticize him for carrying his mat on the sabbath.

What spiritual blindness! What a lack of humanity and warmth! How unattractive religious rectitude can be!

We have already looked at Jesus' reaction here to their criticism of him for healing on the sabbath (see p. 8). His answer: 'My Father is still working and I also am working' is a penetrating one. Jesus links himself with the continuous and re-creative work of God. If you read on to the next passage (John 5:19-24), you will see that Jesus not only makes this strong link, but says that he does nothing on his own, but only what he sees the Father doing. 'Whatever the Father does, the Son does likewise.'

As we wonder at Jesus' healing power and ponder the secret that lies behind it, we should note Jesus' very close dependence on God and his strong faith in God's continuing work of recreation and healing. Jesus strongly encourages us to believe that we too can be linked with the powerful life-giving Spirit of God and do works of healing. If we turn to John 14:12, we will see that Jesus says, according to John, that if we are 'in him' in the way that he is 'in the Father', we will do the works of healing that he does 'and in fact do greater works than these'—a staggering promise.

For Thought and Discussion

1. Reflect on the question 'Do you want to be healed?' and its implications.

2. Discuss the problems of long-term illness. What kind of ministry is appropriate?

3. Some might think that Jesus' promise that we would do greater works than he did is too extreme. What do you think Jesus meant by adding 'because I go the Father'?

20

The Touch of Healing and Compassion

Reading: Mark 1:40-45

Jesus, in his healing ministry, often used the ministry of touch. He laid hands on the sick as an outward sign of blessing and healing from God. Luke's gospel tells us that 'power came out from him' (Luke 6:19), while in another place Luke tells us that when the crowds gathered outside Peter's house seeking healing 'he laid his hands on each of them and cured them' (Luke 4:40).

We are told that Jesus was deeply moved with compassion for the leper who came right up to Jesus and knelt before him, saying: 'If you choose you can make me clean'. Jesus reached out and touched him. Lepers were regarded, and are still regarded, as untouchables, banished from human society. This leper broke the rules; he came right up to Jesus and knelt before him. Jesus also broke the rules by reaching out and touching him. This act of Jesus must have meant an enormous amount to this diseased and alienated man.

Mark's account has a curious word in it, though it is not in all early copies of the gospel. It says that Jesus 'was moved with anger' when he saw the leper's condition (perhaps not only his physical condition, but his human alienation). Perhaps Jesus was angered by the man's suggestion that he might not want to heal him. So early copyists of Mark's gospel probably changed the text to say that Jesus was moved with compassion, rather than anger. Matthew's gospel tells it that way. We are told that Jesus' heart went out to people on a number of occasions in the gospels. He burned with a compassion that came from a very deep place in him—'in the gut' is the way the Greek language puts it.

Laying on of hands is an outward expression of conveying God's healing power. It can also be seen and experienced as a touch of God's love and care for the individual person. We have already noticed Luke's description of this individual attention which Jesus gave. Many people can attest to an experience of well-being, even a flow of healing activity in their being, when hands have been laid upon them by others. There is a sense that we are cared for and loved. The outward sign expresses that we care deeply for the one being prayed for and that together we are calling on God's healing power for him or her.

Care should be taken not to lay hands on heavily because such treatment can be distressing for the person being prayed for. For those doing the ministry, we do not believe that we are accomplishing the healing, but rather God is the one in whom we trust. Too much concentration and effort on our part may serve only to block the flow of healing and draw attention to ourselves.

Notice in the story of the healing of the leper—as well as in the healing of the ten lepers recorded in Luke 17:11-19— that Jesus tells the persons to go and show themselves to the priests. This was a traditional way of certifying their healing and a pathway for re-admission to society when the danger of infection had passed. The modern equivalent would seem to be that any of us who feel, after receiving healing ministry, that we are cured, should first go to the doctor who has been treating us, to be examined and to have the healing confirmed, before we forsake our medication or speak about our healing.

Notice also that the leper who was healed ignored Jesus'

instruction not to tell anyone and went out and began to proclaim it everywhere. He must have been a powerful witness because the crowds flocked to Jesus so that he couldn't go into a town but had to stay out in the country.

For Thought and Discussion

1. What has been your experience of the laying on of hands either as a giver or receiver?

2. Discuss the value of outward signs of healing being used. Are there any dangers?

3. What place should be given to testimonies to healing in public worship or in the church's publications?

21

Persistent Faith

Reading: Matthew 15:21-28

One of the notable features of Jesus' ministry was his willingness to minister to Gentiles. This may not cause any surprise to us; we are accustomed to hearing that God's loving mercy is available to all people regardless of their racial or ethnic background. In the religious outlook of Jesus' time, however, there was definitely an insider and outsider point of view, rigidly practiced. In the temple precinct, for instance, there was a wall called the dividing wall, with a notice that any Gentile going beyond this point would be put to death. Early Christian writers speak of Jesus breaking down this dividing wall through his death on the cross and of the Gentiles having full access to God's blessing and God's promises (see Ephesians 2:14-18).

When a woman from the area of Tyre and Sidon started shouting after Jesus about her daughter being tormented by a demon, it seems, according to Matthew's account, that Jesus initially gave her no encouragement or help. First of all we are told that he took no notice of her at all; then, when the disciples urged him to tell her to be quiet and send her away, he says that he was sent only to the lost sheep of the house of Israel. This statement, unique to Matthew's gospel, suggests that Jesus did not see his mission to include the Gentiles. However, we are told that the woman came up and knelt before him, saying simply: 'Lord, help me.' Jesus' word to her still is negative: 'It is not fair to take the children's bread and throw it to the dogs.' We shudder when we realize the import of this saying, knowing that the Jews of the time referred to Gentiles as

Gentile dogs (prowling, as it were, around the edges of the Jewish community). Is it possible that Jesus could be so insulting and discouraging to a poor woman in her need? Perhaps he was speaking ironically and meaning: 'this is what people usually say, what do you think?' Whatever spin you put on Jesus' words, the woman's persistence and faith are remarkable. She has a good reply to give—'Yes, Lord, yet even the dogs eat the crumbs that fall from their master's table.'

Jesus then commends this Gentile woman for her great faith and affirms the answer to her persistent prayer. Her daughter was healed at that very moment.

This is not the only occasion when Jesus commended a Gentile person for showing great faith. In the case of the centurion who comes to Jesus and asks him to heal his servant, believing that Jesus needs but to say the word and he will be healed, Jesus remarks that he has not found such faith 'even in Israel' (see Matthew 8:5-13). We see in the gospels that Jesus responded to people's faith. He certainly responded in compassion to all kinds of people's needs, but there is the idea that his sense of mission was expanded as he encountered unexpected faith in him on the part of Gentiles. Certainly the early Jewish Christian communities had to grapple with this question and were stretched in their understanding of the breadth of God's love and mercy as they sought to be faithful to Jesus and what he had said and done.

However, these and a number of other healings in Jesus' ministry show that persistent, strong and humble faith drew forth a response in Jesus. As we engage in prayer for healing and acts of healing ministry today, we do well to remember the place given by Jesus to persistent prayer. In the case of the Syro-Phoenician woman, her faith and the genuineness of her prayer were strongly tested. Yet, she was deterred by nothing and her prayer were answered by the complete healing of her daughter.

For Thought and Discussion

1. In reflecting on this passage what impression do you form of Jesus?

2. Reflect on (and perhaps share) times in your life when persistent prayer and faith have been required.

3. Are there ways in which your vision of God's mission in the world has been stretched to cover people not previously thought of?

22

Word and Sign

Reading: John 4:46-54

In John's gospel Jesus' healing miracles are referred to as signs. John tells us that the healing of the royal official's son was 'the second sign that Jesus did after coming from Judea to Galilee'. The official would have almost certainly been from the court of Herod. He lived at Capernaum, a strategic town on the Sea of Galilee. He left his son there and went to Cana to seek Jesus' help.

At first it seems that Jesus discourages the man—'Unless you see signs and wonders you will not believe.' It should be pointed out, however, that the 'you' in this statement is plural; so Jesus was making a general statement to those around rather than addressing the official in particular.

Despite any perceived discouragement, however, the man persists in his request: 'Sir, come down before my little boy dies.' Jesus immediately assured him that his son would live and that he could go home. The man believed the word that Jesus spoke to him and set out for home, only to discover from the servants who came to meet him that his son had recovered from his fever at the very time when Jesus had spoken his word of healing.

We are reminded in this healing event that Jesus could heal with a word. His word had power. 'Word' in the Bible has that sense—it accomplishes that for which it is sent forth. We read in the prophet Isaiah: 'So shall my word be that goes forth from my mouth; it shall not return to me empty, but it shall accomplish that which I purpose and succeed in the thing for which I sent it' (Isaiah 55: 11).

Jesus is giving a sign to the world that he is the one who speaks God's word and truly is the one sent from God. When we engage in a preaching or healing ministry in the name of Jesus, we humbly realize that there is power in the spoken word, especially if it is a word from God. Paul referred to 'the sword of the Spirit which is the word of God' (Ephesians 6: 17).

Think of a wrong medical diagnosis; that is an example of the negative power of a word uttered, and it can affect the whole of a person's life. So a healing word can have a positive effect on our being, especially when we believe it.

Jesus was clearly able to heal at a distance. This encourages us as we join in intercessory prayer, or lay hands on a proxy at a healing service, praying for someone who is not present. It is not unknown that a healing blessing can be released in a person or persons at the very moment when they were prayed for, even though they were some distance away, or were not even aware that they were being prayed for.

Jesus' ministry consisted of both word and sign. He proclaimed the word and the truth of God, but his healing ministry was a sign to those who believed that he truly was of God. The church's ministry today is powerfully authenticated when people's lives are healed and changed in a way others can see.

For Thought and Discussion

1. Why do you think Jesus said: 'Except you see signs and wonders you will not believe' in this context?

2. Recall and share times when you or others have experienced healing at a distance.

3. Discuss this sentence: The church's ministry today is powerfully authenticated when people's lives are healed and changed in a way others can see.

23

'The Kingdom of God is among you'

Readings: Luke 17:20,21; Matthew 12:22-29

Many people of Jesus' time believed that when God's Messiah came to the world he would set up an earthly kingdom. According to the temptation stories, this is what Satan offered Jesus: 'All this I will give you, if you will fall down and worship me.' Jesus' aim was to set up the reign of God in people's lives. His teaching about the kingdom of God was very much about our response to present realities—turning from a life of self-seeking and being converted to God's love, showing mercy and generosity to others, practicing forgiveness, stepping across religious and social barriers.

There is a future aspect to Jesus' Kingdom teaching, but his suggestion is that we shouldn't be rushing off after every teacher who says: 'Look, here it is' or: 'There it is.' Jesus also quite definitely taught that no one will know the day or the hour of the final coming of God's rule and judgment; he didn't even presume to know himself (see Matthew 24:36).

Jesus stressed that the issues of the kingdom of God are to be dealt with in the present, not postponed, as some in the early church communities were inclined to postpone them, thinking the end would come very soon.

Jesus also indicated that his healing and deliverance ministries were signs to people that the kingdom was already present in the world through his works. 'If I with the finger of God cast out demons, then the kingdom of God has come to you.' He had been accused by his critics of casting out demons through Beelzebul, the ruler of demons. Beelzebul means 'Lord of the flies'. It was shameful, to say the least, that some who saw Jesus making people whole and bringing God's peace into their lives in an evident way, ascribed his power to the Lord of the flies, the chief demon.

What spiritual and human blindness! Jesus had some harsh words to say to these 'blind guides'. They were sinning against the Holy Spirit, the Spirit of truth, who was bearing witness in their own spirits to the goodness of what Jesus was doing. Such sin against evident goodness and truth, he said, was beyond forgiveness.

Some believers understand Jesus' words at Luke 17:21 as meaning that the kingdom of God is within us. An implication of this reading of the text is that all the potential of God's blessings is in us waiting to be released or stirred up.

Another reading of the text which is probably closer to the meaning of the Greek is 'the kingdom of God is among you.' Jesus was stressing that the kingdom—the rule of God—was breaking into the midst of the world of human affairs through his presence. In other words, the kingdom is present in Jesus.

So when we pray 'your kingdom come on earth as it is in heaven' we are not only praying that God's kingdom will come in the future when there will be a new heaven and a new earth; we are praying for that kingdom to be realized in our midst now.

When we celebrate the Eucharist together we believe that Jesus is present in the community of faith, just as he was present to his disciples on the first Easter night speaking his words of peace to them, and showing them his hands and side. As we go about our lives we should think of the one who promised us that he would be with us, every day, to the end of time. When we engage together in healing ministry we do so in the presence of the risen Jesus. May our hands and our words be his healing hands and his healing words for those who gather. In that sense, it is good to remember his word that 'the kingdom of God is among you.'

For Thought and Discussion

1. What do you think Jesus meant by the kingdom of God?

2. What different emphases and understandings come from translating Jesus' expression as 'within you' or 'among you'?

3. A prayer after communion in *A Prayer Book for Australia* (page 151) speaks of the church being 'a sign of your wholeness in this broken world'. How does the church become this sign?

24

A Variety of Approaches

Reading: Mark 5:21-43

Those who study Jesus' healing ministry, and the whole range of healing events described for us in each of the four gospels, will notice a great variety in them. Sometimes people reach out to him in faith, sometimes Jesus takes the initiative; sometimes the sick are brought by their believing friends and Jesus responds to their faith; sometimes people make the journey of faith themselves; sometimes Jesus lays hands on the sick, takes them by the hand or gives some outward sign of healing such as using his saliva or spreading mud on the eyes; sometimes he heals by word only; sometimes healing takes place at a distance, other times Jesus goes to be personally present. Many times Jesus tells people who have been healed not to tell others about it, and in at least one case tells the man to go and tell his own people what the Lord has done for him (see Mark 5:19,20). Sometimes Jesus gets rid of the crowds of people, or takes the person aside from the rest, and other times he does the healing in public, with everyone watching. Sometimes there is clearly faith on the part of the recipient, sometimes the healing is a complete surprise.

The more we examine Jesus' healings, the more we are impressed by their variety. Is there a message here for us? We like to have predictable ways of doing things in the church community, and prescribed ways of ministering healing which we follow month by month or week by week. Just as Jesus was able to respond to each person and situation, we should do the same. Sometimes it is appropriate to conduct the ministry publicly, sometimes it is better in private;

requests for healing ministry can come at any time, and at any church gathering. Delay and some preparation might be appropriate, other times it is best to act immediately. Overall, it is important for us to be sensitive, responsive to the person's need, and responsive to the Spirit's leading.

In Matthew, Mark and Luke the account of the healing of Jairus's daughter (Jairus is only named in Mark) is intertwined with the healing of the woman who had suffered from hemorrhages. This latter healing takes place along the way, as Jesus goes to visit the little girl. The healing takes place in the midst of the crowd and the woman does the reaching out for healing herself. The little girl's healing takes place in the privacy of the house, with Jesus making a point of putting all the noisy people outside, and taking only the parents and the inner circle of disciples into the house with him. There are times when we need to take a small band of believers with us to do healing ministry to provide some surrounding faith, and times when this is not possible. Involving the close friends or family of the sick person is also a good thing to do.

In conducting healing ministry today, privacy and confidentiality are important, and every effort should be made to respect the dignity of the person being ministered to. We are not at liberty to tell the congregation about someone's illness, or the fact that they are in hospital, or enlist prayer on their behalf, without the person's permission. As far as bearing witness to healing that has occurred is concerned, we have no right to demand this, yet a strong encouragement to do so may not be out of order. Jesus persisted in looking around on the crowd asking: 'Who touched my clothes?' There certainly is a place for testimony to healing in our public gatherings. Having prayed for the sick by name or having witnessed healing ministry taking place in the midst of worship, it is edifying for the congregation, from time to time, to hear of blessing received. There is no rule about this; sometimes the details can be revealed, but always with the recipient's permission.

For Thought and Discussion

1. Is my congregation, prayer group, chapter, in danger of getting in a rut as far as prayer and healing ministry for the sick is concerned? How can this be avoided?

2. In what ways can we safeguard confidentiality for the recipient in our prayer and ministry?

3. What kind of training is appropriate for participation in healing ministry?

25

Healings in Acts

Reading: Acts 5:12-16

Luke's account of the early ministry of the apostles is re-corded in the book of Acts, also called the Acts of the Apos-tles. The commission of Jesus to the twelve and then to a wider circle of seventy (some early documents say seventy-two) to proclaim the Kingdom of God and to heal the sick is described by Luke in his gospel in chapters 9 and 10.

It appears from these accounts, and from similar passages in Mark and Matthew, that it was clearly Jesus' intention to train and empower his disciples for the work of teach-ing and healing in his name. As with his own ministry, teaching (or proclamation) and healing were to be inter-twined. In John's gospel there is a clear promise that Jesus' disciples, whom he calls his friends, will do the works that he does, and even greater works (John 14:12).

The Acts of the Apostles show how Jesus' commission and promise were borne out in the witness and work of Peter and Paul and the other apostles of the early church com-munity. Throughout this vivid and exciting book various acts of healing and deliverance are performed in Jesus' name. For example, there is a detailed account of the way a crippled beggar is healed at the gate of the temple (see Acts 3:1-16).

As Jesus had apparently intended, these miracles occurred though he was still alive and ministering, bringing people to wholeness of body, mind and spirit. Christians believe that Jesus is indeed alive, and his presence and power are known in the faith and life of the community of those who believe in him.

The passage set for this study has strong echoes of some of the crowd scenes described in the gospels (for example, in Matthew 14:34-36) where many people crowded in to receive healing for themselves or their friends from Jesus. Now the crowds could receive this same healing from the apostles and the apostles' fellowship. 'They were all cured', says Luke, expressing amazement at the signs and wonders which were accomplished among the people through the apostles.

From Paul's letters, we learn that Luke was a doctor and companion of Paul on part of his journeys. As you read the Book of Acts, you will notice that in some places the narrative changes from 'they' to 'we'. You can see this transition if you read Acts 16:6-13. Clearly the author, Luke, had joined Paul and Silas. His accounts of Paul's ministry were in some cases eye-witness accounts.

You will also notice that the early Christian community grew fairly rapidly. We could well imagine that, just as the crowds came together to hear Jesus and observe his healing work, so the healing ministry of the first apostles helped to draw people to their ministry and witness.

It could be argued that the same dynamic would apply in today's world. Healing ministry and evangelism can go together, one complementing the other. The risen and living Jesus can be known through the proclamation and witness of the Christian community. He is known to us in the breaking of the bread and the sharing of the cup. He can also be known and experienced in the ministries of prayer, laying on of hands and anointing, as people come with their needs and burdens.

For Thought and Discussion

1. Search out four examples of healing ministry record-ed for us in the Acts of the Apostles. What was achieved through each of these healings?

2. Do you think that the kind of healing ministry exercised by the apostles should be expected in the life of today's church? Share together the reasons for your answer.

3. In almost all churches there are prayers for the sick. Are there reports of healing or other answers to prayer in your church community?

4. How could the church strengthen its ministry of thanks-giving with respect to blessings received?

26

Gifts of Healings

Reading: 1 Corinthians 12

We can be glad that the Corinthian church had serious divisions over questions of leadership and the exercise of various spiritual gifts. We have some of the Apostle Paul's best writings and teachings as a result. In these early letters we also discover what kind of ministries went on in the life of the early church communities. Amongst these ministries is the ministry of healing.

It is clear from the twelfth chapter of Paul's letter that Paul expected the members of the church to have a variety of gifts and ministries, that not everyone should be expected to have the same gifts, and that they were to be exercised 'for the common good' and in a spirit of unity, not for personal aggrandizement.

Near the beginning of the chapter Paul speaks of nine different spiritual gifts which were manifest in the Corinthian church community—the word of wisdom, the word of knowledge, faith, gifts of healing, working of miracles, prophecy, discernment of spirits, tongues, and the interpretation of tongues.

Some Pentecostal churches teach that there are nine gifts of the Spirit—that this list is a definitive list and should be manifest in all churches. Some even teach that every individual Christian should have the gift of tongues as a sign of their salvation.

Yet it is clear from the end of the chapter that this is not

Paul's teaching. He asks the rhetorical question: 'Do all speak in tongues?' to which the expected answer is 'No'. Likewise, you will note, he asks 'Do all possess the gift of healing?' Again the expected answer is 'No'.

A sensible way of approaching the text is to realize that Paul is giving examples of the kinds of gifts experienced in the church, not giving a definitive list. This approach is supported by examining the gifts and ministries mentioned at the end of the chapter (verses 28, 29). Here there are some extra gifts mentioned: 'forms of assistance' and 'forms of leadership'. It is also clear that other gifts again are mentioned by Paul in other places (see, for instance, Romans 12:6-8).

You will notice from the title of this study that there is a double plural—'gifts of healings'. This is how the original Greek reads. This suggests that not only is there a variety of gifts of the Spirit, but within the area of gifts of healing there is further variety—'gifts of healings'. Our experience of the healing ministry reinforces this variety. Some join in laying on of hands and anointing, some support with intercessory prayer, some provide pastoral care, some are gifted in counseling, some provide helpful suggestions for diet or special exercises. We have already learned in these studies that we are to 'honor the physician' and call for the help of the pharmacist. We know that God has various ways of helping and healing us and imparts his healing gifts in various ways to various people. In contemporary times we have come to appreciate the importance of medical research. Should we not include this in our understanding of the 'gifts of healings' which God gives us?

Paul's encouragement to the Corinthian Christians was to exercise their various charismatic gifts in coordination with one another and in a spirit of unity within the church community which he calls 'the body of Christ'. The different parts of the body need one another; so within the Christian community we need one another and need the various gifts which are given through the different members as we work together in harmony with one another.

For Thought and Discussion

1. Have you encountered situations where the variety of 'gifts of healings' has not been fully appreciated and all the emphasis has been on one form of ministry only? What were the results of this approach?

2. If the gifts of healing and other spiritual gifts are there within the church community, what should we do to uncover and encourage them? How should this affect the way we do healing services?

3. Identify within your group the spiritual gifts which the members have experienced in themselves or others. Pray together for the strengthening and wise use of these gifts.

27

Gifts of Insight

Readings: 1 Corinthians 12:8-11; Hebrews 4:12,13

As well as 'the gifts of healings' mentioned in the last study, there are other gifts of the spirit which contribute to the ministry of healing. Clearly the gift of faith is important. As we confront a particularly difficult situation, a special gift and outpouring of faith may be given to a member or members of the praying congregation as a resource given by God to help us. Though we all need faith, without which we can hardly have a relationship with God, there is, from time to time, an extraordinary gift of faith given to help us as the healing body of Christ. It could be called a deep movement of the Spirit in the area of faith.

In this study, however, let us focus on gifts which give insight. These gifts—a word of wisdom, a word of knowledge, and discernment of spirits—help us in the areas of diagnosis and in the development of self-knowledge, which is often very important as we travel on the path to healing.

In the Letter to the Hebrews, the author tells how 'the word of God is sharper than any two-edged sword, piercing to the dividing of soul and spirit, joints and marrow; it discerns the innermost thoughts and intentions of the heart'. When we are exposed to God's word and Spirit, we see ourselves more clearly as we are, and we believe that he knows us deeply and truly.

Deep insights about ourselves are often painful, but in seeking God's forgiveness and healing in the innermost parts of our being (the parts we hide even from ourselves), we can experience an outward healing as well. His 'Spirit of truth' knows us through and through; there is no deception possible with him. You will notice, in the account of Jesus' conversation with Pontius Pilate before Jesus' condemnation and death, that Jesus says to Pilate: 'Those who are of the truth listen to my voice.' The cynical Pilate asks: 'What is truth?' without really wanting to know the answer (see John 18:37,38). To know the truth, and the truth about ourselves, is an important step toward wholeness. Those who are courageous enough to be the followers of Jesus can face the truth about themselves, with his help.

When a wound is being healed, some exposure to the light and open air is necessary. Infection can set in if the area is covered for too long. This is also true for psychological and spiritual wounds. The uncovering of some old hurt, over which we have had much bitterness of spirit, and its exposure to the light of God helps to bring healing. We feel better when we know we have faced something and dealt with it. When the Christian community prays and ministers to a sick or inwardly troubled person, gifts of insight are frequently given by the Spirit. There may be a word of wisdom uttered, giving a new way of seeing the problem or of handling it. The word of knowledge is often a special insight given, going deeper than intellectual knowledge.

In the words of a healing prayer, or the thoughts that accompany it, very often the recipient of the prayer will be given such insight that they will say: 'How did you know that—did someone tell you?' Yet the person uttering the prayer may not be conscious that such an insight is being given. As we seek to be led by the Spirit in the way we pray, it gives us confidence to know that such gifts are frequently given.

Words of knowledge and insight given to those assisting in

ministry should be handled carefully and with discretion. Check with the person leading the ministry before anything is publicly shared; the dignity and confidentiality of the person being ministered to should always be respected and protected.

For Thought and Discussion

1. Consider what happened to the chief tax collector Zacchaeus when he met Jesus (Luke 19:1-10). What insights did Jesus display about Zacchaeus? What insights did Zacchaeus face about himself? Could the changes in his life be described as a healing?

2. Can you recount any special insights you have had about yourself from this study which have helped you?

3. Have you experienced the spiritual gifts of insight in relation to the healing ministry? Is there some experience you can share with others?

28

Discernment of Spirits

Readings: Mark 13:22,23; 2 Corinthians 11:13-15

As was mentioned in the last study, the gift of discernment of spirits is one of the gifts of the Spirit which brings insight to the people of God as they seek to minister in Christ's name.

In the Hebrew Scriptures it was recognized that some who purported to be prophets of God were not so. They had a 'lying spirit' in them and only sought to mislead or to give a prophecy which was favorable to the ruling powers or for personal gain. The true prophets of God like Jeremiah suffered because they persisted in speaking out the word of the Lord even though it was bad news and therefore unpopular. Jesus spoke of people being deceived by false Messiahs and false prophets who would produce signs and omens to lead astray. Paul spoke of Satan transforming himself into an angel of light in order to lead people astray and of some miracle workers disguising themselves as apostles of Christ.

All this suggests that in the healing and deliverance ministry of the church the gift of discernment of spirits is needed for the safety and guidance of the people of God. In seeking to be channels of healing for God, the use of the very word 'channel' reminds us that there are many who claim to be channels of healing or use objects as channels of healing, but may be drawing on the power and influence of spirits other than the Spirit of God.

Through the gift of discernment we can discover whether

something is coming from God or from a false and deceptive
source. When a church or an individual believer opens up to
the gifts and ministries of the Holy Spirit, interfering spirits
can get in amongst us. Satan can also exploit our human
weaknesses such as the desire for self-aggrandizement,
wanting to manipulate or control others, or some inner
need we have for recognition and acceptance. Notice how
often Satan exploits a party or factional tendency within
the church to bring division and weaken Christ's cause.
God gives a gift of discernment so we can sort these things
out. It is essential in the exercise of any of the gifts of the
Spirit that our hearts are right with God, and this applies
most especially to those who are in leadership. Any lesser
motive than that of glorifying God will not do.

When we are praying for healing it is important to know
the source of the trouble. Sometimes a spirit is involved,
such as a spirit of fear, and we need to take authority over
it in the name of Jesus. This or any other spirit needs to be
discerned. On the other hand, there is a danger in seeing
a spirit 'under every bush', and too much talk about spirits can be harmful and obsessive. Wisdom, knowledge and
discernment are all needed, working together so that a correct spiritual diagnosis can be made. 'Naming' a disease,
or problem, or the source of a problem such as a painful
memory which may have been severely repressed, is an
important step on the path to healing. Have you noticed
how you feel better once your sickness is named? We notice too, in the ministry of deliverance, that the naming of
a spirit is crucial in taking control of it in Jesus' name.

In the ministry of counseling (truly one of the gifts of healing), the counselor and client seek to identify together what
the truth is about the client's situation, with the counselor
helping the client to take responsibility for themselves,
rather than dodging it. The ministry of discernment of

spirits will certainly remain an important part of the ministry of healing and wholeness.

For Thought and Discussion

1. How do you see the gift of discernment of spirits being exercised in today's world?

2. What dangers lurk around the church's ministry of healing and deliverance?

3. Have you known of situations where hurtful memories have been repressed and supposedly 'forgotten'? Should we seek to dig them up?

29

Healing Practice in the Apostolic Church

Reading: James 5: 13-16

In James' letter we are given a glimpse of the healing ministry of the church led by James. It is thought that this letter is the work of James the Lord's brother, who became the leader of the church in Jerusalem, and one who was deferred to as a leader in the early church. In Acts chapter 15 we are told that he presided over the meeting of the apostles and church representatives concerning the admission of Gentiles into the church without their being circumcised and obedient to the detail of the Jewish law. James wrote the circular letter which was delivered to the various churches giving guidance on this very important matter.

In this letter James gives a lot of practical advice for church members. Near the end of the letter he speaks of what they should do when they are sick. He urges them to pray and stresses the value and power of prayer. He exhorts them to call upon the elders of the church (that is, the ministers and leaders) to come and pray over the sick person, anointing them with oil in the name of the Lord. He speaks of the importance of the prayer of faith which he says will save the sick. 'Save' as we have been reminded before, can mean the same as 'heal' or 'make whole'. Confession of sin is also recommended: 'Confess your sins to one another and pray for one another, so that you may be healed' (this time a different word for healing—'so that you may be cured').

Within this relatively short passage there is a lot said about the church's ministry of healing:

1. Prayer is used with those who are sick. This has been nearly universal practice in Christian communities from the beginning.

2. The 'prayer of faith' is mentioned. Jesus said: 'Whatever you ask for in prayer, believe that you have received it, and it will be yours' (Mark 11 :24). James seemed to understand this principle as he speaks of praying for wisdom in this way: 'Ask in faith, never doubting. . .' (see James 1:3-8).

3. James suggests that sick persons should take the initiative themselves not only in praying for themselves, but in calling for the elders of the church to come and pray over them. The surrounding faith and prayer of the gathered community helps to bring about healing.

4. Anointing with oil is recommended. Anointing with oil for healing was apparently a widespread ancient custom. Olive oil is known to have healing properties. Massage with oil has a soothing and healing effect and can lead to relief of pain and stress. We read in Mark 6:13 that the first disciples of Jesus, when they were sent out by him to preach and to heal, 'anointed with oil many who were sick and cured them'. Anointing with oil as well as laying on of hands has been widely practiced in the church as an outward sign accompanying prayer for healing. These sacramental signs help to give a focus for faith.

5. The exhortation to anoint with oil may mean that James was encouraging church members of his day to make use of medicine and ointments, and whatever natural substances God has given us for healing. There is no dichotomy here between the physical and the spiritual.

6. Receiving forgiveness of sin is recommended as a part of the healing process. In other words, we are to seek inner

healing as well as outward physical healing. A burden of unforgiven sin, as we have discovered elsewhere in the Scriptures and in practical experience, can be a barrier to healing. We can be sick in our soul as well as in our body. Both need to be attended to, and one strongly influences the other.

For Thought and Discussion

1. How is the advice given in this passage from James heeded in your church community?

2. Do you ask for this ministry yourself? If not, why not? Share any experiences you have had of healing ministry along these lines.

3. How would you describe to someone else what is meant by 'the prayer of faith'?

30

The Vision of a Healed World

Reading: Revelation 22: 1-7

The visions of the last book of the New Testament are of a new heaven and a new earth which God will bring about. They fill out for us what is involved in praying the words that Jesus taught us: 'Your Kingdom come, your will be done, on earth as in heaven.'

Included in the vision which John has of God's kingdom is fullness of life, comfort and healing in the Lord: 'God himself will be with them; he will wipe every tear from their eyes. Death will be no more; mourning and crying and pain will be no more, for the first things have passed away. And the one who was seated on the throne said, "See, I am making all things new."'

Not only is this a vision and hope for humankind which is proclaimed by the people of God; the use of the present participle—'I am making all things new'—suggests that God is already at work in creation bringing it about. So when we engage in the ministry of healing, in whatever way we are led and gifted, we are fellow workers with the healing God who works to save us and makes us and all his creation whole and complete.

St Paul also appears to have had this kind of vision. In his letter to the Romans he spoke of 'the whole creation groaning in labor pains until now; and not only the creation, but we ourselves, who have the first fruits of the Spirit, groan within ourselves while we wait for adoption, the redemption of our bodies' (Romans 8:22,23).

When we engage in the ministry of healing, we may have many discouragements, but we are aligning ourselves with the working out of God's good will for his whole creation. God is a healing God who creates, re-creates and is able to make all things new. God is doing this all the time. The one who made us in his own image has planted healing processes in our bodies, minds and spirits. In God's name and power we want these processes to be stirred up in us and through us. We want to be channels and agents of his healing purposes.

In the final chapter of the Book of Revelation we are given a beautiful vision of the new heaven and the new earth. The river of the water of life flows through the middle of the street of the city of God. On either side of this river is the tree of life (reminding us of the expulsion of Adam and Eve from the garden of Eden and the inability of human beings to have access to this tree and its fruit as a consequence of their sin; now in God's restored Kingdom we can have access to this tree and its fruit and leaves). The tree is not only a symbol of life and growth in God—'eternal life' or 'abundant life' is the way Jesus put it, according to John's gospel; it is clear that the tree is a symbol and means of healing—'the leaves of the tree are for the healing of the nations.'

What a vision of healing and restoration we are given! It is an inclusive vision. All the nations are able to stream into the city of God. Its gates are never shut and people will bring into the city what is unique and special to them. It is a multicultural vision. Only those who persistently sin and practice falsehood are excluded. In the vision it says that the nations will be healed and will all walk by the light of God. 'His lamp is the Lamb'—Jesus, the light of the world and the lamb who was sacrificed for us all is at the center of this vision with God.

With this glorious vision before us, our series of studies comes to an end. We have sought to grow in our understanding of the healing ministry from the insights of the Scriptures and from reflecting on the ministry and teaching of Jesus and the apostles. We should never lose sight of the ultimate hope and vision we are given at the end of the Bible—a vision of healing and hope for all people. God wants you and me, in our time and place, to be channels of his healing and restorative work. May the Holy Spirit help us to be just that.

For Thought and Discussion

1. Is there a danger in our ministries which focus very often on individual need of our losing sight of the wider work of healing—the healing of communities and nations? How can we guard against this danger?

2. Read Ezekiel's vision in Ezekiel 47:1-12. What are the similarities and differences when comparing it with the Revelation vision? What healing references are there in Ezekiel's vision?

3. Read or sing to one another this blessing (from *Together in Song* 778):

> *Shalom to you now, shalom, my friends.*
> *May God's full mercies bless you, my friends.*
> *In all your living and through you loving,*
> *Christ be your shalom, Christ be your shalom.*

- Elise Shoemaker Eslinger (Used with permission)

Appendix

Our Need for a Discerning Spirit

An address to a meeting of the Order of St Luke in Victoria, Australia, on 12 May 2001

Having recently retired after 40 years in the stipendiary ordained ministry, I have entered upon the blissful state where I have some time to think and reflect upon my life and ministry. On the one hand I have been asked by the National Library of Australia and its Oral History Unit to record an account of my whole life to the present and have completed fourteen one-hour CDs to this end. This has been a very good thing to do for my own sake and for my family's sake. I believe it's been a healthy thing to do as it's given me perspectives and a sense of the grace and providence of God in my life. On the other hand I now have a ministry which includes providing some spiritual companionship for younger clergy, some musical input at theological level and with seminars on the new Australian hymn book 'Together in Song' which I helped to produce. Best of all, my wife Gloria and I have been able to collaborate in providing healing ministry and teaching here and there under the auspices of Order of St Luke the Physician.

What has happened, as far as I understand it, is that various threads of my life have come together to give me a better sense of perspective, and, dare I say, a wisdom about how to do ministry, or how not to do it. In particular, there is a wisdom about when to be cautious and when to be bold, and not to confuse caution with timidity and boldness with presumption.

One change which took place in the course of my life was

a move from caution to boldness in matters of prayer, faith and proclamation. I was reared in an Anglicanism which taught me the basics of Christian faith and helped me to worship, both privately and corporately; I can't remember a time when I didn't go to church and I was fortunate to belong to an overtly Christian family where religious issues were discussed openly and sometimes argued over quite energetically. This Anglicanism sat in the middle of the Christian tradition neither too high nor too low, neither too excessively emotional, nor too rigid and demanding. The Christianity of my parents was practical rather than mystical, and in my teens I was drawn more to the mystical and sacramental side. I went to be organist and choirmaster of an inner suburban church when I was 17 and there this part of my Christianity was accentuated in the sacramental and worship life of this church. The healing ministry, with laying on of hands and anointing, was talked about and practiced. We were taught also to develop our own private prayer life and to be intercessors for others. We were bolder too about witnessing to our faith, having street processions about the streets of Burnley, then an industrial suburb of Melbourne, each Good Friday and rather exciting passion plays and other liturgical dramas in and around the church.

As a result of the influence of this church and its ministry and of certain important friends in the church music area, I wondered whether I was called to the ordained ministry. At the moment when on a Melbourne tram car, I admitted to myself that I was being called that way, I took a journey from caution to boldness—an important step for me.

In fact, as I review my growth as a person and as a Christian I realize that I've had to make that same journey a number of times. For example, when I became a regular preacher after my ordination as deacon and priest, one of my helpful and encouraging critics was my first wife Beverly. She remarked to me one day that I was good at saying on the one hand this and on the other hand that. I still do it. She suggested that in speaking I needed to be more decisive and not appear to be sitting on the fence somewhere in a middle position. At almost the same time I went to a conference where we had to send a telegram to someone encapsulating the good news of the gospel in no more than sixteen words. I realized as I did this that there was always the challenge before me to be able to preach the gospel rather than talk about the gospel, so that people could hear it rather than hear me. I was learning to be bold and simple even though I knew deep in me that that is quite different from being brash and simplistic.

At the end of the 1960's I was drawn into a local chapter of the Order of St Luke. When I became a Chapter Chaplain I was often in the position of having to lead in prayer and ministry. This required some stepping out in faith with few visible means of support; I likened it at the time, I remember, to walking out on a plank and diving in. I've never been a good diver at the swimming pool, and I had a recurrent nightmare as a child that I had to walk out on a pier, the pier being invisible below the water line. I can still recall the mental picture and the feeling of alarm with which I would wake up. I did however learn to be bold and direct in my praying and to listen to what the Spirit was saying, and as well to heed pictures that came to my mind as I prayed for particular people. Time and time again people experienced blessing and healing and being known and cared for by God. I learned that there was such a thing as a word of knowledge—God's gift which came in the midst of ministry with people I didn't necessarily know. This happened so often through the specific feedback that people gave me, that I realized that his gift really does flow as we minister and believe together.

Encouragement and help came from visiting speakers on the OSL network. Len Harris from Sydney and David Chambers from New Zealand came by to visit the chapter and give teaching, and I began to attend OSL Conferences. A remarkable person came through from the London Healing Mission, a Church of England priest named, appropriately, Parsons. Roy Parsons had a powerful and Spirit-filled ministry and it moved me to tears as I saw Jesus healing through him and was privileged to minister beside him. I saw tears running down my cassock, and asked myself why I was weeping. I was weeping because what I believed about Jesus, but more as a reality 2000 years ago, I now saw happening before my very eyes. This definitely helped on the journey of faith, a journey from timidity to boldness.

One former Warden of OSL I've already mentioned—Len Harris—impressed me by his careful study and analysis of all the healing miracles of Jesus and his apostles. For my own part as I went through one biblical example of healing after another (both Old Testament and New) and teaching about them at one OSL Chapter meeting after another and one healing service after another I could see the variety of ways in which healing takes place. Sometimes there is a healing word uttered, sometimes not, as in the case of those who reached out to touch Jesus' cloak. 'As many as did so were healed' we are told.

Sometimes there is a sacramental action—laying on of hands and simple touching, sometimes there is not. Healing takes place in a number of Old Testament examples through appropriate treatment: a fig poultice, or bathing in healing waters, or mouth to mouth resuscitation. Jesus sometimes makes use of spittle as a healing and antiseptic fluid of our own remarkable bodies. Sometimes there is faith on the part of the recipient or those who bring that person, sometimes there is not. Sometimes healing is connected with the forgiveness of sins, other times it is not mentioned. Sometimes Jesus heals in the midst of the crowd and sometimes he takes the person aside. Sometimes the healing effects an evangelistic purpose as with the man who had a legion of spirits and was delivered and made whole in mind by Jesus—he was told to go to tell his own people all about it; other times the healed person was told to keep quiet about it and tell no one—not that anyone did what they were told. Healing was sometimes for insiders—the lost sheep of the house of Israel—other times it is for rank outsiders. As far as we can see healing was given to non-believers as well as believers, to the worthy and the unworthy.

I also took careful note of Mark 6 where we are told that Jesus was hindered by the unbelief of his own people (perhaps even his own family): 'He could do no deed of power there, except that he laid his hands on a few sick people and cured them. And he was amazed at their unbelief. Even Jesus was sometimes affected by the surrounding faith of others, or lack of it.

One thing I did notice was a certain sure-footedness on the part of Jesus and the apostles or on the part of an Old Testament prophet. There is the guidance of the Spirit given after a time of prayer, or certainly through a heightened sensitivity to the Spirit brought about through having a constant life of prayer. Elijah prayed earnestly, crying out to the Lord, and then stretched himself upon an apparently dead child three times; he cried out to the Lord again: 'O Lord God, let this child's life come into him again.'

Think how many times there is reference to Jesus looking to the Father before he proceeded with healing. When Jesus healed the man who was deaf and had an impediment in his speech, according to Mark's gospel (7:31-36) we are told that he took him aside from the crowd, put his fingers in his ears, and he spat and touched his tongue. Then looking up to heaven he sighed and said to him 'Ephphatha', that is: 'Be opened'. Apart from Jesus' clear actions being an excellent way of communication with a deaf person—the sign language of prayer and healing—does not the sigh indicate to us a deep moving of the Spirit in Jesus? 'The Spirit', Paul says 'intercedes with us with sighs too deep for human words' (Romans 8:26). Clearly Jesus experienced and practiced deep prayer in the Spirit. Those of us who step out in faith in Jesus' name need to practice that same depth of prayer as he did, and look to the Father as the one with whose will we seek to be in tune.

There is no doubt that I needed to travel a certain journey, sometimes a stumbling one, from caution to boldness in relation to practicing the healing ministry in the name of Jesus Christ and with the authority he gives us. I don't disparage caution. It stops us from being too hasty, too presumptive, perhaps even superficial. Listening to the person seeking healing is so important, so we hear the real need. Listening to God through the Spirit is also essential. We admit that very often we don't have the wisdom to know how to proceed. We should also listen to one another in the church because within the body of Christ very often a word of wisdom, of knowledge or of discernment is given.

Matthew's gospel speaks of our need to seek agreement together in prayer—some seeking of agreement (including with the patient, if possible) and then moving together in the prayer of faith. Nor should we try to persuade ourselves about what we believe or manipulate others into faith through the uttered prayer. Sometimes I hear this. It is better to wait on God and one another and then proceed to prayer when conviction comes upon us rather than setting out uncertainly, and rambling about in the prayer. In fact you will notice that healing words and healing prayers in the Bible are brief and to the point. Faith is expressed in inverse proportion to the number of words used, in my experience. Use simple language, faith-filled, but brief and direct. Make plain statements of faith: 'Lord you are present to heal. Stretch out your hand and touch Joan. Make her whole in body, mind and spirit. Release her from pain and set her free from fear in Jesus' name, Amen.' Amen means 'yes' and we might remember Jesus' plain words 'Let your *yes* be *yes* and your *no* be *no*' (Matthew 5:37).

I'm helped by James' words about faith and prayer when asking, for example, for wisdom. 'If any of you is lacking in wisdom, ask God, who gives to all generously and ungrudgingly, and it will be given you. But ask in faith, never doubting, for the one who doubts is like a wave of the sea, driven and tossed by the wind; for the doubter, being double-minded and unstable in every way must not expect to receive anything from the Lord' (James 1:5-8). The same James, in speaking about the healing ministry in words most of us OSL-ers have committed to memory, speaks of the prayer of faith which saves (i.e., heals) the sick.

However, faith is not to be confused with will power. The prayer of faith is resting in God, not screwing up our wills. Faith is seated in the Spirit, not the mind. It is a resource of the Spirit. I'm reminded of Lady Macbeth's words to her husband: 'Fail? Screw your courage to the sticking place and we'll not fail!' Courage and determination are admirable qualities in those who are needing to be healed and self-help is not to be despised. However, it is not to be confused with faith. So sometimes when someone says: 'I have a lot of faith to get well' they may well mean: 'I have a lot of will power to get well.' The trouble with will power is that it lets us down—we can't control our own healing and often it is beyond our understanding. Depending only on will power can make us feel guilty and a failure when we can't achieve healing. Exercising the will also tightens us up rather than relaxing us down. An important step in healing often is the admission that we can't accomplish it ourselves and accepting the help that is offered. Sometimes we need to arrive at a position where we make a kind of self-surrender and admission of our need. Many a recovered alcoholic can testify to this, where will power has failed. By way of passing comment, it appears that gambling addiction is becoming more and more common in our community following the multiplication of gambling outlets in every locality as well as at the big casinos. We may well need to develop an effective ministry of healing in this area, and certainly support those engaged in counseling work in this troubled area.

Let me return to the important need for a spirit of discernment in our ministry. I refer to the importance of discerning where the real trouble lies in a person's condition. Then we need a discerning of the person's continuing need to be treated with respect, dignity and with confidentiality as ministry proceeds.

We certainly need agreed faith as we meet together to pray and to minister; we also need wisdom and discernment to know the way the ministry is to be conducted, and a strong dose of continuing love for and sensitive care of the person we're ministering to. To manipulate persons in their state of need is a form of abuse. The ministry is certainly not to be a demonstration of our power, but of the Lord's mercy.

We often turn to 1 Corinthians 12 to remind ourselves that God has given gifts of healing to his church and no doubt expects us to exercise these gifts. The original Greek of the text actually refers to gifts of healings (plural) which suggests that there will be various kinds of healings experienced in the church's life and ministry. The text suggests that there may be various gifts of healing just as there is a variety in the whole way of the Spirit's working—so much so that we never pin it down or neatly explain it. That's a sobering reality. I note that in any given sickness where we are asked to minister it is never quite clear whether it was the prayer of faith and laying on of hands, or the right medicine, or the surgery, or the continuing intercessions of a prayer group, or the encouraging love and care of relatives and friends, or getting the right diet which explains the healing. I also remind you that after 1 Corinthians 12 and the emphasis on the varying gifts of the Spirit including the gifts of healings comes the well-known chapter on love (1 Corinthians 13) where Paul, in a moment of high inspiration says that even if we have faith strong enough to move mountains and have not love, we are nothing. Genuine love for the person we are ministering to must always predominate, and certainly predominate over the results we are looking for or want to bring about.

Recently the Church of England has issued a comprehensive report on the ministry of healing entitled 'A Time to Heal: A Report for the House of Bishops on the Healing Ministry'. I was asked to acquire a copy of the report and write a review of it for Healing Contact. Generally speaking, I respond very positively to this report which strongly recommends that there be a public healing ministry in every parish and diocese of the Church of England. It really places the healing ministry right in the center of the church's mission and ministry. For this leadership we are truly thankful and pray that its many helpful recommendations will be taken up across the life of the world- wide church where we can rightly encourage and equip one another. This is, without doubt, the calling of the Order of St Luke. Again, by way of passing comment, I want to say that I do not agree with those who say OSL should go out of existence when the healing ministry comes into the various churches. I believe there will always be a role for OSL, as a ginger group, constantly reminding the churches of the importance of this ministry. More than that we exist as an ecumenical group to promote healing ministry as a ministry we have in common, and to help equip and encourage one another in seeing to it that healing ministry is carried out in a responsible and theologically sound way. I think most of us have encountered people who have been damaged by unsound healing ministry which has been sometimes abusive and manipulative, and has left people in a state of burden and condemnation because they 'didn't have enough faith', or wouldn't deal with a purported 'blockage' to healing.

Now it is true that blockages do get discerned and wise and sensitive ministry can help a person deal with them. There is a time to confront and a time to refrain from confronting, as any good counselor would know. We in the Order of St Luke try to promote a responsible, loving and sound way of proceeding with healing. We want to be bold in faith, but certainly not presumptuous, or invasive of people's own privacy and personhood. There will always be, I believe, a need for the Order's presence and ministry with its history of ecumenical experience in healing ministry.

To return to the report 'A Time to Heal', I want to say that on first reading it I thought there was too great an emphasis on the need for training for those who engage in the healing ministry. There is the hint, here and there, that only trained people should be involved. There is more than a hint of the need for control and regulation from above. Now this may reflect a tendency towards institutionalism on the part of the Church of England. The report is addressed to the House of Bishops so I suppose that the focus is on making recommendations to those leaders. Certainly we would welcome the encouragement for them to take initiatives in appointing advisers and seeing to questions of the training and equipping of clergy and others who are going to engage in the healing ministry.

In our Australian way we may not welcome control, regulation and guidelines, or too much cautious hedging around of the healing ministry. I found myself reacting to the suggestion that at the local level no one should proceed with any deliverance ministry at all without the supervision of the diocesan advisor. It also suggested that in the case of a request for this kind of ministry we should first refer the person to their doctor—either GP or psychiatrist. Now this is a bit much. The doctor or psychiatrist may not be at all interested in the question of deliverance or exorcism, in fact may be totally hostile. That is not to say that the person mightn't need such ministry. There is a lot to be said for supervision by experienced ministers in the exercise of deliverance ministry when that is done, but many of us know that within the course of what we might call 'ordinary' ministry of healing at a healing service or in prayer counseling ministry there is a need to take authority over rebellious or harmful spirits such as a spirit of fear, or a spirit of avarice, or to break an obsession which has become seated in the person's psyche or spirit.

We sometimes refer to dealing with 'oppressions' rather than 'possession' in what could be called lighter cases of deliverance ministry. One would hardly ask people to go and ask their doctor for advice first, in every case. Yet I can see and have experienced the value of help from psychiatrists and psychologists too in dealing with deep-seated obsessions. I would recommend a 'both/and' approach here, encouraging the person to seek professional help where this seems to be needed. It is a dangerous area, one must admit, but I would have to say that some prayer for healing, under the guidance of the Spirit, turns appropriately to a form of deliverance as it often did in Jesus' ministry – the one who set free those who were bound.

To be fair to the Report, it is appropriate to have guidelines and some cautions in relation to the practice of healing ministry and in particular the practice of deliverance ministry. We should take care not to get out of our depth, not to proceed without the help and supervision of those who are senior and experienced in such ministries and for all of us to have people to talk things over with.

We also have a tradition in the Order of St Luke, and a right one too, of honoring the role of the practitioners of medicine and psychiatry. I do not believe in using the word psychiatry as a dirty word as some Christians are inclined to do. Psychology and psychiatry deal with sicknesses and distortions of the mind and the more scientific understanding there is of the mind and disorders in the psyche the better. We do, however, bear witness to the fact that there is a deeper level of our being than the psyche—the realm of the spirit where there can be disorders of a very deep kind. We are not afraid to enter into this area, as part of our calling and ministry, but certainly not without the help and advice of others and well covered by prayer. We also should 'honor the physician' and the pharmacist, too, as we are bidden to do in the Book of Ecclesiasticus (also called the Wisdom of Jesus Son of Sirach), a book which was almost certainly recognized as a holy book in the time of Jesus.

There have been some conspicuous examples in our own country, and elsewhere too, of the dreadful result of exorcism ministry when this has been carried out without appropriate safeguards, without any recourse to medical advice. In most cases the ministry has gone on and on, and can be classed as a form of serious physical or emotional abuse. Some of these so called exorcisms and crazy ill-informed treatments have ended in death, and people have rightly been charged with manslaughter. In 'heavy' deliverance ministry we need to set appropriate limits and act with caution rather than a reckless boldness. This is my point: we need to be aware when we are moving into what could be called presumption and putting ourselves in the place of God. No matter how much we believe in God and in Jesus Christ, who reveals God, and the Holy Spirit who guides and leads us, we remain fallible creatures of God, who make mistakes and fail to listen to God, blinded, perhaps, by our determination to win through and prove we've been on the right track. There is a time for stepping back and admitting that we are in deeper water than we know.

Let us constantly humble ourselves before God—I Peter speaks of 'humbling ourselves under the mighty hand of God'. I'm sure that this disposition is very necessary in relation to healing and deliverance ministry. We have to acknowledge that, without God's grace and wisdom and without his gifts of knowledge and discernment, we are likely to go astray and be not only ineffective, but positive-ly harmful.

The Church of England Report refers several times to a program which is now running across many parishes of the country where there is deliberate aim to train church members in listening skills. An English friend who is un-dertaking this course has promised to send me details of it. She was most enthusiastic in describing it to me. I believe that this is very important for us members of OSL We need to be good listeners, to God and to those who come for ministry. When needs are stated and requests for prayer made we should listen carefully to what is being said (or not said). Half listening and then jumping to conclusions or understandings is a fault of many of us. You will notice that Jesus listened to the cries of the human heart. We are told that he knew what was in everyone (John 2:25). He was observant and he listened. He asked questions like 'What do you want me to do for you?' even when the person's need seemed obvious. Another time he asked 'How long has he been like this?' so he could hear the full story before he began to minister. He sometimes took the person aside from the crowd so he could concentrate on the person's need, and perhaps in order to listen to God himself. Certainly he sought times apart for himself, so that he could discern the path ahead. This may not have always been obvious to him. If this was true for him, all the more for us.

I trust that all of us can make a journey from timidity and excessive caution to some boldness in praying for healing and claiming God's promises for us. I presume we wouldn't be part of OSL if we had not made this journey. However, we will always need the Spirit of discernment in ourselves and in the body of Christ so that we know when to be bold and when to be cautious; certainly we need to discern when we are being presumptuous—when we are going beyond our limits, or not listening to wise counsel. As well as being subject to Christ, according to Paul, we are to be subject to one another.

According to John's gospel, Jesus also spoke of doing nothing on his own. 'Very truly, I tell you, the Son can do nothing on his own, but only what he sees the Father doing.' We are not to do things on our own and without God's leading or without submitting ourselves to one another—that indeed is presumption. In our Chapters and in our healing services let us pray for the stirring up of the gifts of the Spirit amongst us—words of wisdom and knowledge, gifts of faith, gifts of healing, especially the gift of discernment of spirits. There are other gifts too, not necessarily mentioned in that first list in 1 Corinthians 12. We need gifts of leadership, of teaching, good counsel and of deep compassion and love.

Apart from the expectations we have as we meet in Jesus' name and as his people, all that I have been saying indicates that we need a long-term commitment to growth in wisdom and discernment. This can only come from a persistent life of prayer and meditation on the Scriptures, and of course from many actual experiences in the healing ministry. There is no substitute for either of these twin pillars of wisdom.

About OSL

There are many methods today that claim to bring healing into our lives but as Christians we know and understand it is only in and through Jesus Christ the great Physician and Healer that we can obtain that wholeness of life that is God's gift to us. It is being faithful to teaching and practicing the healing ministry of our Lord and Savior Jesus Christ that is at the core of the work and mission of the Order of St. Luke.

To learn more about OSL and how you can join us in our Lord's ministry of healing, please refer to our website: www.orderofstluke.org. You may also send an email to our business office at OSL2@satx.rr.com. Or you may call our toll-free number (877) 992-5222 in both the United States and Canada.

We look forward to hearing from you.

The Ven. Lawrence W. Mitchell
North American Director
The International Order of St. Luke the Physician

Group Study

Readers can extend and deepen the work of this book by organizing and leading a group study of its content. To place an order for additional copies of this book, or to inquire about a group purchase, or to receive information about other volumes in this series, please write:

Speedwell Press
PO Box 131327
Roseville, MN 55113
USA

You may also send us an email:
publisher@speedwellpress.com

Or you may visit us online:
www.speedwellpress.com

Members of OSL may also order copies of this book from the OSL Resource Office by phoning (877) 992-5222 or by emailing oslresourcecenter@satx.rr.com